"...this collection explores the psychological and neurophysiological roots' of the mistrust of the 'other'...with...a lot of heart. In other words, these essays aren't strictly conceptual or intellectual exercises, but rather very personal attempts to reconcile the contradictory, almost religious belief in an inherently superior nationalist identity with simultaneous mistrust in our American institutions, both of which are often enacted within the author's own family. Somehow, despite its direct engagement with incredibly fraught issues as gun control, gay rights, xenophobia, and far-right conspiracy theories, as well as more esoteric ideas such as phenomenology, it's also incredibly readable and often very, very funny. In the title essay, for example, the author slyly adopts the manic, circular rhetorical pattern of a conspiracist as they describe the various outlandish theories to which members of their own family have subscribed. If I were a bookseller, I'd shelve *iWater and Other Convictions* in a special display that contains texts that don't fit neatly in the academic or personal essay sections, perhaps in a section curated to generally thinking, feeling, curious human beings."

~ Xhenet Aliu, Judge, 2020 Steel Toe Book Award in Prose

"In this collection, Robert D. Kirvel explores the power and the limitations of language. In a time when the ability to clearly communicate with others, to give voice to ideas with well supported evidence, to understand how language can both burn bridges and build them, Kirvel asks the reader to listen and to ponder and to come to some understanding. In his essay, "A Bomb in the Final Essay by Oliver Sacks," he shares this thought: "To this day, I ponder, as you did in your last essay, the implications of living with no eraser, as the outnumbered do, while coping with the indelible." Whether it be writing or speaking or reading—the moment of thoughtful consideration is of utmost importance. Kirvel reminds us of this and thus reminds us of our shared humanity."

~Jill Gerard, Editor, Chautauqua

iWATER
& OTHER CONVICTIONS

ROBERT D. KIRVEL

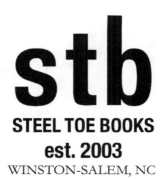

STEEL TOE BOOKS
est. 2003
WINSTON-SALEM, NC

iWATER
& OTHER CONVICTIONS

Merion,

Your art plus my words:
tangible evidence of
our friendship.

Love,
Bob

For the outnumbered
gone or present
in spirit

Contents

Introduction

... nothing in the world ... has as much power as a word
—Emily Dickinson

Most of us want to be understood and valued, and awareness of what is of value often comes through telling and listening to stories. This book of stories and essays is about people we all know, including friends and acquaintances who embrace unfounded and extreme opinions, or who are drawn to untrustworthy sources of information when making decisions. Of course, it's one thing to put stock in pyramid power for amusement, another to risk one's life on false cures or to compromise the planet by denying empirical fact. How can we account for what feels to many people in the Western world like a contemporary epidemic of uncritical thinking that glorifies hogwash?

iWater and Other Convictions is a hybrid collection of essays and *sui generis* prose focused on exploring the numerous ways—subtle to blatant—subjective and personal opinions (human convictions) are shaped by highly charged political, social, sexual, and philosophical concepts. Catalysts compounding the problem include loaded words people use that tend to co-mingle fact and illusion. In contrast to scholarly treatises, the aim of this book is to entertain, move, amuse, and sometimes provoke readers who would like to make more objective sense of shifting social–psychological expressions of opinion. A central theme is the idea of personal authenticity versus its absence. The book has five parts.

Part 1 is an extended metaphor satirizing how our perceptions of a presumed threat from the outside world, and involving people closer to home, can color and distort personal interactions. The allegory about imaginary iWater serves as a point of entry to larger questions about culture, technology, and human connection.

Part 2 begins to show how an ostensibly personal burden, such as the author's identity as a gay man, can be transformed into strength through critical thinking and expressions of psychological authenticity as opposed to the converse: polarized thinking and manifestations of inauthentic bias. Other topics include ways to interpret stances on several contemporary, hot-button issues, such as gun control, abortion, religious and political certitude, xenophobia, intolerance, and more.

Part 3 highlights the potency of language—sometimes in the form of a word or whimsical phrase—to influence beliefs. Even unconscious word choices are capable of elevating our kind of people ("us") at the expense of other people out there ("them").

Part 4 offers intriguing explanations derived from psychological research to help explain the wildfire spread of self-deception and mass delusion along with some new ideas about how empathy operates in the brain. Such work provides insight into why popular and widespread views, including conspiracy theories, so often miss the mark.

Part 5 considers what it feels like to be "erased" as an individual by coping, or failing to cope, with conditions such as dementia, AIDS, the recent COVID-19 pandemic, victimization, and loss of a loved one. A final essay suggests the possibility of personal emancipation from fear and an awakening, if only in the imagination.

Complementing our desire to understand and be understood by others, stories can shed light on our convictions. Nothing in the world, as Emily Dickenson knew, shapes our thoughts and beliefs—from utter foolishness to certainty about the value of critical thinking—more than language itself.

Part 1. A Metaphor For What Ails Us

iWater

No matter what the present success in straightening out difficulties ... problems
will recur in the future in a new form
—John Dewey, *Morals and Conduct*

Aunt Lois had always been Aunt Mabel's doppelgänger, but on a January morning that swapped frigid temperatures for ordinary expectation, the housemates physically fused flesh on the front seat of their shared Toyota with the engine still idling, heater switched off, and radio tuned to a SiriusXM rap station. It must have been the percussive force of hip-hop blasting at sunrise from Bose speakers that drove a neighbor to call the police. Responding patrolmen reported finding the half-frozen bodies of two handholding, look-alike nonagenarians with not much clothing on, so that EMTs had to peel backsides off the vinyl seats like so much Velcro. Nobody in the family could account for the music.

If the relatives had fancied themselves respectful of other lives and choices by trusting in the great equalizer, fate, any remnant of human agency went out the window that day. It wasn't really about the tunes of course, no matter police fixations. A range of domestic attitudes began to skid as well on that glacial winter morning, but was the weather to blame, a failure of contemporary sociological constructs, or something else?

A day after the wake, Uncle William, younger brother of Mabel and Lois but no spring chicken himself, got on Craigslist and bid on a 1975 Porsche 911G coupe. He took a taxi to the bank to withdraw large-denomination bills, slipped the wad inside an envelope as if in a trance, slapped the envelope into the hands of the seller, and drove the Porsche home to park it next to his practical sedan. Uncle William stood a few paces back to regard the purchase, noting how the lemon yellow exterior and black Colgan bra gave his acquisition all the pizzazz of a zippy yellow jacket. Why did he do it? It wasn't as if he stood to inherit a chunk of change from his dead sisters.

A penny-pinching cousin wagged his nose. A niece notorious for practicality clicked her tongue. In-laws, pursing lips and aiming horizontal fingers at nothing in particular, figured the combined estate of the elderly aunts would total somewhere in the "low diddlysquats."

Across town William's firstborn, Bill Junior, spouted off about how anyone can do anything they please these days. Just that simple. Anybody can say or write anything, and it's all just somebody's opinion, no better than his own. To which his wife, Jen, replied, "Sometimes I feel as if I could pick up some grubby little bug just listening to you, Bill." Jen borrowed the line from a British detective show on cable she'd been watching but felt it hit the mark.

Other family members opined that Bill Junior was probably spending too much time listening to talk radio and surfing the Internet, and that's how he was getting the idea anyone can say or write anything. Not from books. Because on Facebook, you can say anything or, more accurately, post practically anything, and Bill did not read books praising sensible measures such as validity or reliability. Bill Junior just nodded and said, actually, yes, maybe I am surfing the Web a lot, and, furthermore, those ideas about Arctic ice melting and police brutality is (sic) actually made up too because, "Police aren't brutal, people's brutal." Bill had a habit of letting verbs get away from nouns and both get away from reality. He also tended to use "actually" to excess.

William the elder, still licking Porsche wounds over slurs from kinfolk, went out in late spring and bought a top-of-the-line SUV with prosthetic, extrasensory, night-vision sensors for braking in case you were headed at a brick wall at 40 miles per hour in the dark. Even if a driver fell dead asleep at the wheel during a lunar eclipse, the gadgetry would stop the vehicle cold 100% guaranteed in crash tests 40% of the time according to the sales pitch. Plus 13 airbags—just in case—strategically located around hand-stitched, lavender capra seats for gallivanting around town on run-flat, space-age alloy wheels, which William aligned next to the 1975 Porsche. Now neighbors could see not one or two, but three vehicles parallel parked in the driveway: yellow, black, and white, same colors as the flag of Lower Silesian Voivodeship, Poland, though William claimed no Polish ancestry.

Something else was going on about colors a few doors down. Most of the family agreed that Jen, formerly respected for caution, crossed the line when she showed up at Gerald's house one morning and walked around back to coat his just-sprouting Big Boy tomato plants with blue latex house paint without saying boo or what for, and ended up inside her second cousin's pajamas, caressing Gerald's you-know-what with her you-probably-can-guess.

After showering and driving to his office in the Department of Forestry and Water Resources, Gerald sent an e-mail to his superiors about a sample from the Browning District he'd forwarded to the State Laboratory. He'd expected the tests to come back negative as always— routine, no change—but they didn't. Anything but normal. Gerald recalled some advice attributed to Socrates to the effect that, *The beginning of wisdom is the definition of terms*, so he got on the Internet and had a look-see.

*Ayahuasca [n., ah-yuh-**wah**-skuh] the Banisteriopsis caapi vine containing a mono-amine oxidase inhibitor (MAOI). Also called yagé when brewed, the hallucinogenic alkaloid is used as traditional spiritual medicine by indigenous people of Amazonian Peru.*

Peru? Hmm, Gerald thought to himself. What the—?

After dialing the Centers for Disease Control and Prevention (CDC) in Atlanta for the fourth time, Gerald finally connected with the Head of the Water Research Division. What was going on here? Hmm?

"I think there's been a misunderstanding. I didn't tell your State Lab people it was Ayahuasca. I wrote on the reports it was something *like* Ayahuasca. We don't know what it is, but we're working on it."

Dissatisfied, Gerald daydreamed during the afternoon of distribution lines from the Browning Reservoir and of pretty little Jen. When he got home, his wife, Lindsey, screamed that Little Jimmy had been caught posting remarks again about how Feminazis and retarded lesbians should be skinned alive, as if Little Jimmy had ever laid eyes on either flavor of person except maybe on social media, but now the school was complaining and Gerald's brother, George, had called to say that Jimmy was a sexist brat and why weren't his parents watching what was happening right under their noses and under their own roof? Plus other mean and unbrotherly remarks nobody needed to repeat.

When he couldn't make even the second loan payment and the dealer threatened to repossess the luxury SUV, William figured he'd go ahead and file for bankruptcy, what the heck. To which Iris, Lindsey's sister, said that nobody was accusing anybody, but who did William think he was, fooling with those fancy-ass cars of his, which nobody didn't need in the first place? And furthermore, those lazy-ass wetbacks and unwed mothers out there were sucking the economy dry, regardless of ethnicity, but everybody knew what race they were. Lindsey figured the frustration Iris expressed reflected upset over a third pregnancy of her, Iris's, unemployed and unmarried daughter who was drawn—in polite terms—to unskilled and unemployed males of questionable character.

Well, so it was not altogether unexpected when William posted his famous remark on Iris's Facebook page, and Iris unfriended Betty. Nobody was surprised either when Betty slammed the door in Lindsey's face after she came over to lecture Betty again about eating gluten and red meat that was killing the air with all those cow farts and causing global warming—or at least a big chunk of climate change—and where the devil was Betty's Christian conscience anyway? Lindsey did not get to say everything she intended because Betty slammed the door before Lindsey could get out another insulting sentence. A good thing too because everybody knew a person didn't go around questioning Betty's faith if you wanted to remain on your feet and, furthermore, *careless words can make people love you a little less*, according to Arundhati Roy who had written a book Betty happened to be reading.

That summer, according to the timeless rhythm of Mother Earth and the Almighty's glorious firmament above, *the sun found itself extinguished every evening and re-ignited every morning*, as Heraclitus liked to say (circa 500 BCE), even as bickering across backyard fences reached a fever pitch over who had—or might have, or had not—hopped aboard the bandwagon of baloney. Yet despite Sol's predictability, mid-summer daylight itself seemed diminished by layers of atmospheric and mental corruption that unhinged tongues. Gerald noticed it. Uncle Bill did too of course. It wasn't so much a meteorological smog in the air that clouded reason, but a disposition carried on the wind, the suggestion of something malevolent charging the sky and invading the cortex, a tempest of emotional discontent originating from just over the horizon to broadcast emotional thistles and shoot poisoned arrows, denting, darkening, damaging the soul.

Lindsey broke her left ankle in front of the house in early August, and Betty just stood there and snickered like the world's most loathsome sister-in-law. Little Jimmy came home with a broken nose from a squabble during soccer practice over shouting "fag" at somebody, and even mild-mannered Gerald, Jimmy's pop, lost his patience several evenings in a row.

Another mass shooting in Alabama ended with the slaughter of several dozen Army boys who had been donating spare time at a church fundraiser, and Bill posted a photo the same day of a gun's inky muzzle pointed out the page at the viewer. Several thought the image and caption Bill wrote, "Just try it, towelhead," disrespectful of both the living and newly dead. Then when Betty yelled at Bill Junior at the annual Labor Day cookout, Jen dumped the entire crockpot of baked beans on her—Betty's—sneakers, and Lindsey left in tears, hobbling to the car as fast as that bad ankle of hers would carry her. Some days Gerald felt as though he were navigating on hands and knees a landscape of splintered dreams and shattered glass. Tinkle. Tinkle.

It must have been after the cookout that Bill Junior started talking about something or other in history we were better off forgetting, but even if we knew about it, it hadn't happened. That's what he said. The Civil War never happened. Actually, he said, you couldn't believe anything that went on more than a hundred years ago—give or take a hundred—ever really happened at all because, well, who knows? History never happened, period. To which his wife, Jen, upped the antagonism ante with, "You are plain nuts, Bill. Nutzoid."

*

In late September, people start calling it what it seems to be. A sickness.

Just before they show up to repossess the vehicle, Uncle William decides to test the extrasensory braking system on his big SUV, so he drives the thing into a wall and severs several cervical spinal nerves—levels C2 to C5—after impact with some 0.75-inch-diameter rebar. After which he dies and Bill Junior scoffs that false marketing and global warming is (sic) a plot of them liberals, everybody knows that, and he, Bill, intends to get hold of a friend who knows this Middle Eastern guy in the ghetto—er, city—and buy a sh**load of ammo for his 17 handguns and 8 unlicensed assault weapons because if the government thinks they can actually get away with taking everybody's guns away from his Second Amendment Rights, well, those socialists are about to find out that nobody is giving up their guns to anybody no matter what those panda-loving a**holes think in Washington D.C., USA. Period.

It isn't just talk either. Eleven times in a row Lindsey feels the pressure on her chest—*thup, thup, thup, thup, thup, thup, thup, thup, thup, thup, thup*—followed by a pause lasting maybe a minute. Then another series of rapid-fire *thups* sends shrapnel through the air just above the tree line, heaven help the birds a mile or two downstream. She walks around back to see what's up and finds Bill, having unloaded wooden crates of ammo from the pickup, is testing his new anti-tank artillery munitions or whatever you call them. Moments later he barricades himself inside the garage and sits down to work some more on his manifesto about history amounting to a pile of hooey. When the police get a frantic call from Lindsey (that busybody hussy, according to Betty and Jen), they dispatch a SWAT team followed in no time by a van with two correspondents tripping over themselves and a film crew panting for a lead story to feature on the evening news.

The story only appears on a single, local TV station because turmoil seems to be spreading like avian flu courting tuberculosis, and with so much upheaval to cover, regional anchorpersons sound as confused as their audiences out there in TV-land. Disorder is reported not only in the vicinity but statewide, and not just throughout their home state but also in other states. Buildings are burning downtown. An elementary school somewhere or other is trashed. In fact, about the only thing on Eyewitness News channels that night is what people are beginning to think of as "The Madness" with a capital Tee and capital Em.

There are whispers. Ugly rumors. It is the first time an on-air commentator resorts to the expression "End time." Survivalists prick up their ears and head for hardware stores.

"This is an outrage," one silver-haired Senator from Pennsylvania despairs, though he doesn't specify to what his indefinite referent refers.

"It's an assault on American values," a congressman shouts to a mostly empty House of Representatives, where absent members do not have the courtesy to call in sick any more or to offer thoughts and prayers.

"Enough is enough!" newspaper columnists demand of their readers.

Politicians might be heard spewing more incendiary rhetoric, but many of them are relaxing in restaurants and private clubs across the land, sipping flavorful Domaine Leroy, Latricières Chambertin Grand Cru and comparable vintages courtesy of military–defense lobbyists who sniff a windfall on the … wind.

"It's in Lake Mead and the Folsom Reservoir in California." This is what Gerald learns from the so-called CDC expert. "It's in the Mississippi River and Lake Erie. It's everywhere. It's in bottled water."

"Bottled water?"

"Sure. Even bottled water comes from water, you know."

Oh geez, Gerald thinks to himself in his office. "We're screwed," he whispers into his new smartphone that comes with a hefty upgrade surcharge for the first 12 months, to say nothing of hidden fees.

"Some people are calling it iWater. Pha!"

"Pha? What's that mean?" Gerald asks the CDC guy.

"Just don't jump to conclusions. That's all I'm saying."

Ink slingers concoct Star Wars narratives, and though calmer voices of acknowledged scholars urge restraint, nobody mentions Thomas Mann's (*Death in Venice*) observation that, "...*there is nothing so distasteful as being restored to oneself when one is beside oneself*," the author having a terrific way with words even when at his most Germanic and depressing.

"Have you noticed," little Jimmy asks his best friend at school, "how my dad has gotten a little ... ?" Jimmy cannot finish the question properly because he doesn't know the right word to use, being a child of the public education system in America. The word is "paranoid." The next morning, Little Jimmy hides in the attic behind some boxes, trembling at the idea his high school coach is about to come a-knocking on the front door any minute with a butcher knife in hand, hungry for a pound of flesh from "that little s**t-fu**ker" who is causing so much havoc at school. Or maybe the boy's anxiety has more to do with the fact that Jimmy just watched the original version of Alfred Hitchcock's "*Psycho*" last night while sipping several glasses of high-fructose-spiked Kool-Aid. Who's to say?

*

Prayers evidently go unoffered or unheard, and only one explanation makes sense in the minds of those who struggle through it. Aunts Mabel and Lois freezing to the beat of rap music? Or hip-hop, or whatever? What's up with that? Uncle William's sudden attraction to luxury cars and Bill Junior's disavowal of history? Jen's idea that tomatoes ought to be blue? Little Jimmy's phobic bigotry? Obsessions with firearms and the erosion of personal liberties?

iWater.

It isn't real of course, Gerald hears on the phone, but then, "The situation is also worse in some ways than you think," according to the CDC man who tells Gerald iWater is shorthand for ISIS-contaminated drinking water. And although Gerald senses a contradiction and feels certain the expert from Atlanta is privy to inside information, and maybe he is forced to speak in riddles for national security reasons, the man only repeats his personal opinion that the actual culprit, the real deal is, (quote),

> ... a metabolic byproduct of a widespread algal bloom.
> That's my thinking at the moment,

(unquote), whatever that's supposed to mean.

Homeland Security honchos and epidemiologists agree, according to attractively groomed TV personalities who identify themselves as "subject-matter experts," despite having never completed a course in the biological or physical sciences. Chemical warfare has officially gone global; a designer drug with hallucinogenic and possibly neurotoxic properties concocted in a secret lab—probably located in a god-forsaken cave in Asia and definitely, absolutely, certainly funded by terrorists—has found its way into the drinking water supply of America. Well, not "found its way" so much, but has been intentionally dispersed in fresh water throughout the Land of the Free by black-hood-wearing lunatics who would destroy Our Way of Life!

Is it infectious? Who knows and who cares because it's in everybody's drinking water for heaven's sake, which is the President's fault. No question. Pharmaceutical companies are in profit-making cahoots with banks, and the BLM is run by a bunch of know-nothing intellectuals. Homeless people started this epidemic of hatred, positively, plus those illegal vermin getting handouts and screwing all over the place like rabbits. But does any of it even matter anymore? The stuff doesn't kill you; worse, iWater drives you mad and makes you see things that are not there. Like climate change. Like the theory—which is to say, hoax—of evolution, or like the idea of guns killing people when every fool knows they don't. iWater makes you think things and smell things like prairie flatus on the rampage.

A person can go without food for weeks, but not without water. Everybody knows that. Every god-fearing citizen of the United States of America stands to become infected. No, *is* infected, like those Indians way back in the olden days when we gave them the plague or something worse even though nobody meant to do it deliberately, and all that crap is a lie anyway made up by those rich-bastard, casino-owning redskins sucking paychecks from the pores of honest working men and women fighting to make a decent living across the country and getting taken to the cleaners by outrageous taxes. Disgusting.

*

Now it is 8 a.m. sharp on the first Tuesday in October, and the CDC expert updates his assessment for Gerald. More talk about algal blooms, resulting from above-normal air temperatures and high levels of dissolved nutrients from farmland fertilizers in all eight U.S. climate zones specified by the IECC. Gerald scribbles notes ending with a series of question marks.

"The IECC? You mean this is about global warming? What are the medical symptoms when ingested then?"

Mr. CDC does not spell out the acronym or address the climate-change question and simply answers, "Diarrhea."

"That's all? That's it?"

"Essentially."

Gerald slips his notes in a desk drawer and folds hands behind his head. What to believe?

Because *words have no power to impress the mind without the exquisite horror of their reality* (Edgar Allan Poe), mid-October brings a new round of observable revulsions. Churchgoers and agnostics give each other sore throats out on the streets, yell in all caps on Facebook, or blame fiends and savages somewhere out there or down the block. Housewives deplete supermarket shelves of canned soups high in pre-ISIS water content, and bathroom tissue for that other problem, while hubbies stockpile machine guns in closets. Chinese restaurants from the Dakotas to Arkansas go belly up following rumors of "those Asian pagans" deliberately doping with laxatives their lo mein and egg foo young. Gangs of teenage white boys take to burping out loud on city busses and snorting at their cleverness.

After decades of gridlock in the United States Congress, elected legislators take a break for a photo op to stand proudly as One Nation, shoulder-to-shoulder on the steps of the U.S. Capitol Building—liberals to the left and conservatives on the right—with a contagion-proof gap of six feet down a symbolic no-man's-land middle. Lapel pins in the shape of American flags glint in the sun, and just as a photographer is about to snap the historic picture, statesmen standing toward the center reach across the gap to shake hands with former antagonists from across the aisle. Click, good shot. United we stand.

At 6 p.m. Eastern Daylight Saving Time on November 2 (yes, it's still Daylight Saving Time in November, thanks to those idiot bureaucrats) the nation's citizens draw a collective breath of anticipation as the official announcement is made on TV about iWater. Millions of registered voters order another round in bars because you can still trust liquor, thank goodness. Hold the ice.

And then the eagerly anticipated words: "... nothing less than total, full-out, unrelenting, nonstop war!"

Hallelujah. Something peace-loving patriots of every stripe can get behind. Let's let those heathen cowards from Dromedary-Land try to hide from us now under their burqas or hijabs or whatever. Shove it, iWater. Just you wait and see.

That evening, the nation's giant defense contractors throw a shindig a stone's throw from the Senate Office Buildings, and everybody who is anybody shows up. Senators and CEOs. Representatives and governors. Wall Street billionaires and lobbyists—everyone except the country's foremost expert on water contamination, that guy from the CDC, but he isn't anybody any body cares about anyway, so what the heck. Cheers.

Gerald phones the Atlanta offices repeatedly each morning but gets a busy signal. When an administrative assistant finally answers at week's end, she says the Water Research Division Head has taken indefinite family sick leave.

"What's that mean? How long will he be out?"

"Indefinitely, hon."

Gerald walks down the hall to the interdepartmental kitchen and grabs a tall glass from the cupboard, not just any glass but the tallest one. He fills it to the brim with cold water straight from the tap. Bottoms up.

Part 2. The "F" Word

A Bomb in the Final Essay by Oliver Sacks

He challenged a conformist profession as a renegade yet experienced almost pathological shyness in his personal life. He struggled through a near-suicidal addiction to amphetamine. Many remember the man's brilliance and humanity, his gift for forward thinking, and I ask myself two questions. Why were we both inclined to look back and re-inhabit the turbulent terrain of youth? What is it about the enduring impact of that landscape that so many people fail to comprehend? Answers to the two queries have roots in shared and unshared experiences, respectively.

In a last essay, "Sabbath," written just before his death in 2015, the celebrated neuroscientist Oliver Sacks recalls the day he told a parent he liked boys. After confiding in his father and requesting that the revelation not be shared, Sacks's mother was nonetheless informed almost immediately. She reacted with conviction.

"You are an abomination. I wish you had never been born." The condemnation prompted an 18-year-old Oliver to contemplate "religion's capacity for bigotry and cruelty."

After reading Sacks's *On the Move* and that final essay centering on his personal life, I was struck by the range of parallel life experiences. As gay men, we shared with most of our LGBTQ complement the angst of revealing ourselves to family members, courting acceptance and risking annihilation, but we both then led "an almost monkish existence," as Sacks expresses it, until making "... a full and frank [public] declaration of [our] sexuality." We were drawn to brain research and completed degrees in the neurosciences, relocated to San Francisco after graduate education, though decades apart, developed a recreational-drug habit for a time, and ultimately embraced technical and creative writing as avenues for professional and personal expression.

I knew I was gay—the amatory disposition long before the adjective—by age seven but refrained for nine more years from initiating that conversation with anyone, anticipating that if I hadn't aligned with mainstream urges by "sweet" sixteen, I never would straighten out. After telling my mother the secret—fessing up to a semi-phlegmatic father seemed overwhelming—I nevertheless urged her to convey the fact and then relay Dad's response. After a week of silence on the matter, I learned from my father via Mom that I was going through a phase. It would pass. Years on, after going public with other family members, my parents despaired of being the last to know.

"That's what really hurts us more than anything else: your not being honest with us."

Is it possible my affective dynamite, detonated at a tender age, did not register and leave residue? Is it credible to suppose my mother and father simply forgot what I'd said as a teenager? Is denial capable of vaporizing mental engrams, as another neuroscientist, Karl Lashley, liked to call memory traces encoded in the brain?

Sacks wrote numerous books detailing his groundbreaking discoveries related to brain function and behavior, some of which were captured in the film *Awakenings*. But why would a brilliant physician and maverick renowned for compassion and insight, recipient of numerous honors, friend of the famous, choose to exhume a shudder-inducing experience after nine decades of life, and why do I revisit similar territory in fiction and nonfiction?

Much of the answer is revealed in a single word. Outnumbered. It's all about how it feels to be one. One what?

Outnumbered. Once stuck in that remote territory, one does not easily become unstuck from affective alienation.

Sacks stifled sexual expression for decades, suffered from those inhibitions, and responded to religion with disappointment verging on detestation. My reaction was similar, expanding the negativity to wannabe humanists and politicians who fancy themselves practitioners of holiness by quoting—loosely—from the Old Testament that a man who sleeps with a man shall be put to death. The good doctor and I developed a reaction to religious literalism while also eschewing promiscuity, but we knew something in addition about compassion roused by exclusion: how it feels to exist within the flesh as a minority bastardized from without by judgment. How does it feel exactly?

An erotic awakening can shed some light. I had the same teacher during conjoined second, third, and fourth grades, a black woman of exceptional talent who masterfully managed her whippersnappers in an "enrichment" classroom. When racial epithets were lobbed beyond the corridors of kiddy academe and within family circles, I inevitably wondered as a little shaver how Mrs. H might react to them. Then, when sometime during her tutelage my sexual identity announced itself not with a whimper but through an implosion of feelings unnamed but incontrovertible, I wondered more fixedly. My teacher was a minority and so, apparently, was I, but what did that mean?

Of Mrs. H's rules, one was strictly enforced. All erasers were verboten except for a large, green affair that served as her personal power tool. You don't make progress through concealment, and you don't always come to terms with your own mistakes after applying an eraser: that's what Mrs. H told us before offering a more operational explanation.

"I have the only eraser because I want to see your mistakes. Every one of them. When you make a written mistake, I will examine the error with you and remove it with my eraser. That way we shall learn from one another."

In her classroom, one finger in the air, or two, signified one type of bathroom urgency or the other, which was acknowledged in due course by a silent nod plus a hall pass. A catalog of other rules and expectations, reinforced by Mrs. H's upbeat personality, softened the daily academic grind.

A substitute teacher filled in for several weeks when Mrs. H fell ill one November, and my classmates and I learned the two women were opposites in temperament: one high-strung and the other calm, abrupt versus patient, confrontational rather than supportive. There are people who can never be still, inhabit and transmit misery, twitch and shriek when a whisper will do, people who wear stiff woolen outfits that require a jerk or shrug to alleviate an itch that cannot be soothed. Miss B was that person.

Rare events redefine a life, and the Tuesday before Thanksgiving ripened into an experience like none other because I could never afterward think of myself in the same way. If one day altered my sense of self, it also induced, I now judge in retrospect, an emotional abrasion that would find expression as an intermittently recurring paralysis of thought. That feeling is difficult to convey in a word or phrase— by "outnumbered" or any other modifier—but facts can speak for themselves.

Miss B blamed her mood swings on a bad back caused by lumbar compression, or at least that was our substitute teacher's expressed position on the matter of her health. Had the complaint been put to a physician such as Sacks, odds might have favored a diagnosis of personality disorder rather than neuropathology, but in any event her first action when she appeared before us on a Monday morning was to reprimand the impertinent boy who stood up the instant the morning bell sounded to announce he was ready to give a talk (a twice-weekly event scheduled by Mrs. H months in advance). After silencing that disturbance, Miss B told the children in each grade where to begin their lessons, but immediately she encountered unholy rebellion.

"No, Miss B, we already did that one, we're on page 132," a runny-nosed fourth grader whined.

"We're supposed to be in the reading circle next," a third grader told the teacher.

Not one to brook impudence, Miss B mounted a counterattack. "Everyone put your hands down and keep them down until I ask you a question." With that, she pressed fists to temples and collapsed onto her swivel chair.

Through midmorning, no one received permission to talk, and when a hand went up, then another, Miss B spoke to the walls as though they were able to comprehend what unruly children could not.

"Did I ask a question? I did not. Hands down I said."

At 10 a.m. the classroom took on the hush of a mausoleum. At 10:15, the precise time recorded by Dick S. in his fourth-grade notebook, a barely audible sound of something leaking was heard in the room. Miss B hesitated in mid-sentence from what she had been telling the third graders. Was that the sound of running water? She looked around to identify the source of distraction and found it.

"What—whatever are you doing, child?" she snapped. "Stop that! Stop it this instant!"

The trickle escalated into a waterfall as my friend Doreen D sat peeing in her chair. At that moment, the most stupendous sound heard in the building originated from urine striking floorboards. Twenty-three pairs of young eyes rolled like so many ball bearings on a down-slope in Doreen's direction and came to rest on the cascade under her seat. The expanding puddle found a channel between floorboards where lint and bits of debris floated downstream buoyed on the electric yellow current. No child could turn away from the spectacle; no one dared think what might happen next.

Miss B hovered over Doreen, waiting, waiting. At last she demanded, "Child, why didn't you say something?" Her rasp grew louder. "Well now?" Louder still, "Will someone kindly get a mop?"

No one budged.

"I am not in the habit of repeating myself," the teacher bellowed. "A mop!" she repeated nonetheless.

The boldest fourth-grader rose to fetch the implement from a janitorial closet and returned to help tidy up. Doreen remained in the chair, sodden, until lunchtime and did not return to school that afternoon.

Several of us boys met in the school playground just before the first afternoon bell rang. On this day, Dick S offered his technical assessment about what had happened.

"Girls are sissies."

Perhaps because no one responded, he followed up with, "I could have sat there all morning."

I am pleased to recall his small audience walked away, and no further remarks were made at Doreen's expense. I like to think most of us appreciated Doreen's accident might have happened to anyone.

The substitute teacher remained at the helm for two more weeks, during which time my classmates arrived at several insights. For example, when nerves got the better of her, Miss B dabbed herself with one of several handkerchiefs secreted about her person. During a bout of agitation, a hand might go groping sideways within her blouse, this way and that, dislodging a breast or the pair until fingers found linen. With it she dabbed her nose or an earlobe though selected anatomical targets never appeared to be moist, and when fingers returned to her blouse to shift things around while re-depositing the hanky, we understood we must remain absolutely still.

Yet toward the final days of her tenure, tension unaccountably eased, and Miss B was observed to smile a few times on the Tuesday afternoon before Thanksgiving vacation, an occasion imprinted within my skull. The room needed holiday decorations, and in a mood of downright euphoria given the baseline, the teacher clapped her hands for attention.

"Everyone get out your art supplies and draw something with a Thanksgiving theme." Several children asked for clarification, still hoping to please.

"Yes, yes," Miss B responded, "turkeys are okay. Pilgrims are fine, anything like that."

From a reference collection near one of the encyclopedias, I pulled out an illustrated volume and thumbed through scenes of Iowa in winter, desolate landscapes in black and white. I paused at the artwork of someone named Thomas Hart Benton who drew lanky characters on hills sprouting balloon-shaped trees, but what finally caught my eye was a watercolor of two handsome Iroquois in a forest vibrant with autumnal colors. Were they wrestling or doing battle? No matter, I could sense the strain of their body musculature and liked the sensation. The artist's name was not provided, but the image seemed appropriate to a Thanksgiving theme. After all, Pilgrims and Native Americans had struggled and then come together for a feast according to revisionist history.

As everyone else worked, my focus remained absolute. I had an eye for perspective, and the pictures I'd drawn in the past were pleasing, if nothing special. But something unexpected happened as I began sketching outlines of the two Native Americans this day. I experienced the sensation of being able to transcribe feelings to paper, and the marks answered back. In the absence of an eraser, I started with only enough pressure on an extra-hard lead pencil to leave faint impressions. The technique allowed me to refine body contours and adjust scale, and the constraint of working with no eraser forced me to attend to the details, as Mrs. H had frequently advised. Something about the imagery, the anatomy, stimulated my eight-year-old physiology in a thrilling way, causing blood to pulse in fingertips and temples.

In a burst of pre-holiday largesse, Miss B gave everyone permission to walk around the room, if they did so quietly. Boys and girls who finished their work rapidly made the rounds to see what others were doing. They came upon pictures of rainbow turkeys and men wearing belt-buckle hats, cutouts of autumn leaves of every shape and hue, sketches of festive dinner tables heaped with corn and squash. Several children gathered behind my chair.

"Gee, that's something."

"Best one in the class. Bet you're going to be an artist."

I'd never thought about it, but yes, perhaps I would make art one day. Roaming children returned to their seats when Miss B commenced a tour of our handiwork. "Very nice," she said as she collected illustrations one at a time. "Excellent. Oh, I like that one."

After approaching my table from behind, the substitute teacher stopped. I did not see her jaw stiffen as it must have done, but I heard the crackling whisper.

"Young man, we do not have that kind of thing here!"

She might have stuck my finger in an outlet. I glanced at my drawing while experiencing mental paralysis beyond the reach of time though the feeling probably lasted seconds. Had I misheard?

Miss B bent lower until her fuzzy upper lip touched my ear. "Do not give me that innocent expression! You know exactly what I mean."

Her breath smelled of pickles and swamp gas, and my stomach rolled somewhere under the table. She snatched my drawing and stuck it on the bottom of the stack as if to bury an atrocity while whispering something else under her breath, something I could not quite catch although she repeated it. Something about a bomb.

Bomb? What bomb? Had the woman lost her mind?

As she advanced unsteadily to the next table, I experienced an even odder sensation. Shock perhaps, or fear? No, something new. More than scholastic disapproval, her reaction embodied personal condemnation. I had apparently violated a code, but what code? Was there an unspoken standard in art everybody knew but me? Worse than doing the unthinkable was not grasping the forbidden.

Miss B tacked the drawings above the blackboard, except for mine, which I never saw again. While slipping into coats at day's end, classmates toured their holiday creations, comparing one work with another. Dick S noticed the omission.

"Where's yours?"

I shrugged.

"What's that supposed to mean?"

"She took it."

"What?"

I shrugged again.

"It has to be somewhere." Leave it to Dick S, budding empiricist, to insist on all things logical.

"She didn't like it."

A dog with a bone, good ol' Dick would not let go. "What are you talking about? I don't see it anywhere."

"I guess she didn't want to put it up."

"That can't be right. It was the best one."

"I don't know," was all I said, but more than anything else I wanted to escape the third degree because what I did know troubled me more than what I did not. I took my fractured confidence home.

Upon her return to the classroom, Mrs. H heard all about our substitute teacher, but no one mentioned Doreen's mishap, and I did not talk about the drawing in class or at home. How could I explain? I knew right from wrong—or so I'd always thought—but the incident at school went beyond right and wrong, beyond a substitute teacher's accusation and directly to the core of my being.

To little avail I considered logical explanations that might account for Miss B's denunciation in an effort to lessen my dread of exposure and responsibility for having crossed a forbidden line. In adult terms, I obsessed on the substitute teacher's motive. Maybe the idea of hand-to-hand battle suggested by the drawing was unacceptable. Perhaps the male physique captured in my naïvely erotic sketch disgusted her? Such explanations seemed far-fetched and did not account for her censure. And what could that strange business about a bomb have meant? Was there some feature so inherently explosive in my picture that it brought to her mind a bomb? There was indeed. It would be years before her meaning would be revealed to me in the epithet "abomination;" nevertheless, the violation prompting her attack, I knew, lay within me just as a teenage Oliver Sacks felt the interior gravity of transgression verbalized by his mother.

"You are an abomination."

"We do not have that kind of thing here!"

That kind of thing. My take on eroticism, beauty. In other words, me.

I could not get the schoolroom scene out of mental auto-rewind for months, forcing me to relive how the experience felt: in a word, outnumbered. Miss B might just as well have stood in front of the class and announced, "I have been warning children all my life about a certain kind of person, a despicable sort of person." Then with her finger pointing evil at me, "Here is that person." In fact, she'd whispered her remarks so that only I could hear them—and barely hear at that—but her manner of delivery had intensified the impact. Her message was clear. In the teacher's mind, the name of my crime was so foul it must not be spoken aloud. Instead, "A-bomb-in-a-tion," whispered.

Few occasions in life bring with them an epiphany. My first came now. The teacher had looked at a drawing and seen into my heart, found it wanting—more—identified something vile there. Yet in one respect, she was correct: I did know in my gut what she meant. That was the worst part, acknowledging the implications of what I knew. Part of me down deep had always known I suppose, but I had not thought it mattered so much until now. It. Being different. Being aroused in that way. But most shocking was the easy callousness through which exposure could happen. Now, I felt paralyzed by the death of unself-consciousness brought on by a realization that there was something unacceptable within me. Call it character or identity; call it loathsome or what you will. I knew what it was but did not have an adult name for it. Did it even have a name? I'd never thought of myself as so alien from and, more to the point, so unacceptable to other people. To be found out was to be lost; to be called out publicly was to be made dead to hope.

My drawing of two male bodies circumscribed a larger issue from a personal point of view. For the first time, I knew the lacerating effect of a deep-seated conviction expressed by a person with authority. Beyond disapproval, hers was judgment so pure and simple as to be rendered divine, and a judgment from heaven required no explanation. I knew something else too. If I were to do nothing more than breathe in her presence, Miss B would despise me. If I fell prostrate before her and begged forgiveness, she would look down on me and spurn me.

Eager to convict, she exercised the curse of conviction by translating conviction into eviction. Extinction. I, and those of my kind, didn't exist to her.

During afternoon recess a week later, I watched as several older kids harassed a skinny boy on one of the swings. When taunting escalated to shoving, the small boy cringed and tried to get away. "Sissy girl," they called him. With those taunts I relived the emotion I'd felt when I'd been the subject of Miss B's wrath. Although the attack on the playground was the kind of thing every child witnesses, and the action was directed at a kid I didn't even know, it was unwarranted and grotesquely personal. The puny kid, literally outnumbered, lay on the gravel, looking soft around the edges and deflated. Fight back, I thought, though clearly the little guy didn't deserve what he was getting. Just as I hadn't deserved such treatment the previous week. Just as I had not fought back. My discomfort boiled into rage, but just as quickly I put a lid on emotion and watched until the scene played itself out. The lid would remain in place for years.

The older boys tired of the game and ran off, but I stayed within earshot and then walked over to the boy. "They hate me, and they don't even know me," the kid said. Exactly, I thought. Just as Miss B believes she knows something, but she does not know me. This was the first time I recognized an adult to be so right about detecting something and so wrong about conclusions. Despite her ill regard, I also owe Miss B for a defining moment through which I came to understand how to spot from a mile away the insecure. The boy on the gravel and I formed a friendship that outlived his being shot while riding a city bus and lasted until he died of AIDS during the 80s.

Though I would not read Oliver Sacks until many years after the school incident, even in youth the good doctor and I held in common several traits. Both of us came down with a case of premature self-consciousness. Neither had found a voice in conversation or print yet, and it would take decades before we started writing, then a lifetime to explain a truth we knew in our bones.

In grade school I didn't have Oliver Sacks's exceptional adult vocabulary to explain what was genuinely me and not me, at all, but oral skills were unnecessary to appreciate how an authority figure nurtured an irrational prejudice held in common with so many others populating a world in which I numbered among the outnumbered. Contemplating that world of "everybody else" from an emotional place outside it awakened a perspective about separateness, empathy and too often its absence. That disconnection was the first to enlarge my sense of inhumanity and humanity.

So, indeed, I would say to Oliver Sacks, you and I were brothers who shared several experiences unshared by the nonminority population at large, and one requiring a lifetime to surmount. To this day, I ponder, as you did in your last essay, the implication of living with no eraser, as the outnumbered do, while coping with the indelible. I see you with pen in hand, Oliver, on the road somewhere to visit an old patient perhaps, scribbling on paper in the old-fashioned way and thinking about a bomb going off one day in youth. Still exploding now. And now. Forever.

American Exceptionalism

Without monsters or gods, art cannot enact our drama
—Mark Rothko

When on rare occasions we encounter in the flesh the textbook definition of a character type, stereotyping's seductive appeal can feel unsettling. Tad, a shirttail relative, is a good old boy of the my-country-right-or-wrong, love-it-or-leave-it ilk. He donates generously to the NRA, drops everything when summoned for a cause involving bullets, and cheers from his armchair the self-appointed demagogues on biased broadcast and social media because their political arguments are invariably presented, Tad affirms, in such a balanced way.

"I've made a donation in your name to the Flat Earth Society." I fantasize about offering that emotionally fragrant declaration—embroidered on linen and framed—to Tad next Christmas. Yet if better judgment prevails, I will refrain from playing Santa Monster to Tad's inner child because no one, myself included, sees the world as it actually is. Rather, humans experience things as we are, through filters of belief, bias, values, assumptions, and the local culture—call it our personal god-or-monster climate.

It matters: what we say out loud or don't say. Equally affective is how we convey the information.

When I visit Tad and his wife Sonny for a few days during the summer heat, I always remind myself why I've returned to the inland turf of my adolescence. The driving force behind each trip to the west of Davenport, Iowa, amidst 360-degree horizons of field corn is a desire to connect in small ways with recollections of childhood, commune with spirits of relatives departed, and remember my first true friend in life who was murdered in his twenties by a virus—*that* awful virus long before COVID-19. If Tad enjoys hurling buckets of verbal gibberish toward random compass points, his faithful sidekick–chameleon, Sonny, pivots effortlessly with the slop direction.

Awash in currents of mixed metaphors, my mom was fond of saying, *don't cut off your nose despite your face when you get behind the eighth ball.* That she never grasped the game of 8-ball is obvious, but does Mom's counsel about holding versus freeing one's tongue apply to her son when revisiting corn country? Hold that question for a moment.

According to clever biologists, higher intelligence may reveal itself only during a blip in biological time and prove unequal to the challenge of surviving the long evolutionary haul. We have plentiful data to support the idea. Is it surprising then when folks are besotted with the power of astrology and crop circles and Uzies, as Tad and Sonny are? This much, at least, is obvious to me with respect to the topic of firearms: humans as a species are not sufficiently evolved to be trusted with jackknives, let alone guns of any caliber. Stuff your opportunistic interpretations of the Second Amendment, I suggest, along with all the good-intentioned framer–farmers who also believed in the curative power of leeches and a universal incapacity of the fairer sex. There might be defensible exceptions to the losing bet associated with placing firepower in the hands of half-hairy hominids—for example, when a grizzly bear is coming at you— but the adverse consequences for modern times are right there in the numbers. Mom favored another, borrowed notion of responsibility. *So you let the cat out of the bag, so you shall reap.* We reap several thousand deaths by bullet every month. The data are widely reported, so what purpose would it serve to remind someone like Tad of facts?

Part of me knows debate is pointless when two sides are entrenched, especially on a topic as hot as guns. If logic fails, what about illogic then? Or irony, humor, metaphor? Surely something can be gained by exploring a fresh approach when an in-law brings up, for the umpteenth time, the power and glory of concealed carry. But what might that gain be? Something lurking just under the surface about what people say versus what they really mean? Perhaps something about interpretation.

At the breakfast table the first morning of my visit to the land of corn, Tad muses out loud about a legislative initiative he supports: requiring guns in public school. Not just on the part of security personnel or teachers, but children.

"At what age would you like to see kids packing pistols then?"

"Oh, I'm thinking fourth grade." He is serious. "That's what we do now at our church." He nods to Sonny, who nods back. They are both serious.

I speak slowly. "Of course, you are free to conjure visions of deranged jihadists mowing down unarmed kiddies denied the right to concealed carry, if that's your thing, but my thing is classical music and diction." Tad looks askance at me.

"Yes," I tell him, "because—joyful, sad, or bipolar—words suggest affective qualities through their dreams, and who does not like dreams accompanied by a musical score?"

In my head, I explain out loud to my hosts, I often think about the emotional associations of words. I imagine a piccolo enjoying sprightly visions as viola suffers from depression in the dark hours, or I envision a xylophone and flugelhorn acting out episodic schizophrenia in the forest. The truth is that the very mention of concealed carry brings out the worst in me, so I am determined to change the subject by any means possible.

"That makes no sense at all." Tad says. "What you just said."

"What part?" I ask, titillated by the prospect of rapid-fire nonsense and success in confounding the direction of Tad's thoughts. Then I feel guilty for baiting one or both of my hosts.

"The whole thing. All of it. And what you write about too."

Tad waves a magazine in the air over our breakfast sausages, pages open to a piece I had suggested he peruse and from which he might profit, but I was wrong. His swishy wrist motions carry a dismissive quality as he repeats that the narrative, featuring a catgut chorus persecuting one unhappy flugelhorn, makes no sense. Tad's principal complaint seems to be that the writing in question describes as taking place in the real world something that could not happen in reality, including a musical instrument's mental breakdown. Tad is the sort of fellow who enjoys television shows about real people and events: topless vampires, for example, seducing big-hearted hit men, and he likes to repeat plot twists in detail. I counter that the published article under discussion (my own, though I do not remind him) is a metaphor about violation and shame, that some things written may not be true in the literal sense but can capture an aspect of the human condition and elevate our personal understanding. A poem, for example.

Tad says he does not like poetry. His flat intonation leaves no room for doubt. Here is a case of irony if ever there was one, absolutely, if you throw in some irony.

Tad, as fine looking a sandy-haired lug as exists in farm country, can suck the life from conversations and has the habit of interrupting earnest discussions to offer friends a gripping snippet about himself:

"I loved that old second-hand Skilsaw I bought years ago dirt cheap, but one day it quit. When I took it to the guy to fix, he called back and said oil wasn't the problem, no sir, but the air filter had wrecked the compression. I'd been using an air compressor to clean the filter and blew the coating clear off. Time for a new saw. Har, har."

Sonny chimes in with musings about her favorite politician who has written another book in which the principal contentions are that God loves America above all nations on Earth and that Americans are The Almighty's favored children, having never done harm to any living thing in the past or present. She rolls palms heavenward when I mutter something about the danger of positing U.S. "exceptionalism," as Noam Chomsky likes to call it, in light of America's history and ongoing track record of brutal imperialism spiced with the latest iteration of Agent Orange/dioxin or something. Sonny counters that "We, as a Nation" can accomplish anything we want to accomplish, including the destruction of Iran and that other God-forsaken country over there, if we only remember to sing "Onward Christian Soldiers" from time to time. She larks a snippet,

...going off to war, with the cross of Jesus...

to tease my goat. She probably thinks the tune is funny, that she's being funny, and she is in a way. On the serious side, she probably has in mind Stone Age clerics who advocate amputation to solve the irksome problem of bread pilfered by starving urchins. Amputation is bad of course. But is it much better when the citizens of one country fancy they have the right to set right by drone strikes the regressive thinking of citizens of another country about which they know diddly? I silently ask myself the question, not Sonny, remembering Mom's advice. But enough of ammo and Stone Age politics.

*

In the interval between one unguided missile from Tad and the next drone attack from Sonny, I walk far into the fields out back, and my thoughts involuntarily pivot to the nature of the human brain and its equipotential mission. I think initially about coprolites (petrified dung) and chastise myself silently for being ungenerous. I picture a pair of goldfish named Death and Destruction nibbling detritus affixed to recently unearthed archeological skulls soaking in a laboratory vat somewhere in Minnetonka, Minnesota, and rendering the bones immaculate, that image coming to mind because we are, in the end—whether we live with corn, cow dung, or subways—fish food. I think about the reality that I am a visual thinker and a word person and try to imagine what passes for thought in Sonny's noggin. More coprolites sprint cross the visual field of my imagination. Then I remember how some neurophysiologists speculate that religious inclination, interpretable as wishful thinking or otherwise, is an inherent (better term: emergent) property when enough neurons—a hundred billion or so—get together and decide to tame fire and play canasta. So it's really on the inside rather than from the outside that we might look for the origins of belief, is it? Other emergent properties that come to mind during my stroll on the soil are an affiliation with "us" along with an aversion toward "them" (i.e., a tendency to elevate us at the expense of everyone not-us) and a fondness for hot dogs.

*

The television blares in the family room as I saunter through the Iowa farmhouse. The flat screen remains on day and night in this otherwise bucolic place, tuned always to the same "breaking news" station. Another rant is in progress about socialism chewing government to pieces and food stamps digesting economic leftovers.

Sonny quotes from the Bible while looking up at me. "A man who sleeps with a man shall be put to death." Is she joking? Baiting? I suspect the King James Version presented to me during childhood for perfect attendance in Sunday school (thanks, Mom) contains no such recommendation. Then I remember. Am I in handcuffs? I am not. Am I free to go? I am free to go.

Free to reminisce as well while revisiting home turf. After my mother's final consultation with a young surgeon, she cried as I drove us both home, terrified of another hospital and the risks associated with surgery at an advanced age. Her spirits rebounded in the car that sunny afternoon after my telling her what she wanted most to hear: that she need not have the operation if that was her choice, and it was indeed her choice, I insisted. *I think the pigeons have come home to roost* is the way she put it that day, suspecting—as I knew with assurance following an aside from the physician—that death was the likely outcome either way, surgery or no. No irony was in sight that day, except for a brief stint of freedom in the face of death. She was 93.6 years old when she died in my house a few months after the medical consultation—more precisely, died in her wing of my house—in her own bed next to her husband of 65-plus years, about the same terminal age that her Grandma Comstock had attained, our stern upstate New York ancestor with the gold-rush name and fortitude of a Wagnerian handmaid named Brunhilde. Only after Mom was gone did I grasp the extent of unswaying maternal encouragement exceptional mothers award their children. Now there's genuine exceptionalism for you, independent of nationality.

*

Sonny was out back petting her roses when a related thought washed over me, the most hurtful words anyone has ever spoken to me.

"You could have done something. You've ruined my life."

The accusation was snarled by my father, who had convinced himself I'd killed Mom and taken all his money, this after renovating a wing of my house so both parents could spend their final years in a serene setting with their own ground-floor rooms. Five years after Mom died, I did need to place Dad in a residential care facility after all, despite opposite intentions, because of his progressive vascular dementia. "You have no choice," two docs and three nurses insisted following yet another trip to the ER. I rejected, then acceded to their advice when I came home from work one afternoon to inhale acrid air, find molten metal on his stove, and discover our shared washing machine had been crammed with so many blankets and sheets that the repairman needed heavy equipment to extract them. Later that week I found my father on the floor of his bathroom at 2 a.m., sorting pills into cardboard boxes for an imaginary trip, while repeating with urgency that "the people upstairs" (in a one-story home) were ready to go.

Many seniors are not easy to handle toward the end, and my father, who had always kept emotions under lock and key, became downright difficult. Still, after watching the quantum increments of his mental deterioration, a step-wise descent on the rungs of a conceptual ladder to living hell, after cleaning trails of detritus from bedroom to bathroom, upon feeding a parent with a spoon and living with flickering hopes and dying expectations, I know things about the end game others may not care to know. Dad, younger than Mom by about 5 years, breathed his last at the age of 92.5.

*

My soul mate, Norm, asked me just after he was informed of his terminal diagnosis whether I would be all right. "Of course," I shot back reflexively, meaning I'd been okay before we met, and I would be fine for the rest of my life after he departed too soon this plain of sunbeams and terror. Brave words those, spoken as much to reassure myself as Norm, but no dice. The more his health failed, the kinder he became, in contrast to my father's withering temperament. Each time Norm comes to me in dreams, I am overjoyed, then crushed upon awakening to the conscious reminder of an insurmountable loss.

*

Glancing out the sliding farmhouse doors now, I see Tad and Sonny in the rose garden embracing as young lovers would in a Franco Zeffirelli movie featuring a sumptuous musical score that charges autonomic nerve endings. Tad has his hands on Sonny's still-slender waist; she, one palm on his chest, reminds me why I've come back to this place for a reconnection with memories. In this moment, I love them again, both of my parents, Tad and Sonny as well, because love is eternal, if intermittent. Tad drops to his knees and hugs Sonny, with his splendid head of hair pressed against her thigh, an expression so submissive and tender, yet commanding and lovely, that it makes me feel uneasy to watch. Sonny pulls her husband to his feet, and they walk along the rose path in slow motion as if it were possible to remain in physical contact for an eternity of cloudless blue yonders in Middle America.

I would grant them cerulean tomorrows too, particularly after recent tribulations. Sonny has always drawn as much assurance from religion as Tad from his political convictions, but both dispositions were tested by their son, "The Kid," who walks, partly upright, a tightrope of social disequilibrium. When, during my own youth, the family went to a grand auditorium in the city for some special outing, my father always purchased front row seats in the balcony. Even if main-floor sections were available, he insisted on steeply inclined views. I remember trying to fight impulses of hurling myself over the railing and plunging to death, and when struggling to brace back—pushing moist palms against armrests—some mysterious power seemed to yank me forward into "The Downward Path," just as some cerebral force-field apparently tugs at The Kid.

During one visit to Tad and Sonny's house a while back, I happened into the family room to discover the television was not tuned to the usual station. While Sonny fussed with dinner at the kitchen island and Tad scanned an *Old Farmer's Almanac,* The Kid had apparently been given permission to watch a ghoulish movie about college students stranded at a remote cabin in the forest. The boy seemed transfixed but, as usual, remained silent. Then at a moment of crimson theatrical violence, The Kid burst out with the type of wicked laughter that redefines creepiness.

I glanced at the parents, but neither apparently noticed, and I remember thinking—for the first but not last time—something was off-kilter in this house.

I began to see comments The Kid was posting on Facebook about strong women, "retarded" lesbians, and feminazis. Remarks about the myth of rape in the armed forces followed, along with ridicule of transsexuals and venom directed toward obviously disturbed females outside the mainstream who took to blustering on the Internet about unequal pay and other "feminist lies."

"He's sweet," Tad and Sonny kept saying, a thoughtful 14-year-old who keeps to himself. He's an intelligent 15-year-old who doesn't harbor ill will toward anyone.

After seeing more cold-hearted recommendations from my nephew about burning people alive, I responded to his comments online from across the miles, hoping he might think twice before ridiculing others on the Internet even if the intent was a joke. Was it a joke? New posts appeared during his sixteenth year, ignorant and mean-spirited. I sent him a personal email and then another, reinforcing the idea that words matter. Misogynistic rants followed, and I sent a third email to The Kid together with suggestions about some good sources to read: Gloria Steinem on feminism, Carl Sagan's baloney-busting toolkit to draw upon when encountering phony baloney. I urged him to consider joining a debate club at school to learn principles of fair-minded exchange. I wrote Tad there was something we should discuss regarding his son, but Dad never responded.

A few months later, I opened Facebook and saw that The Kid "liked" a blog posing the question, "If you could rid the world of one thing, what would it be?" The blogger answered the question in all caps with, JEWS, and The Kid added his recommendation: "Fags and trannys (sic)."

The world stopped spinning as I struggled to see a way forward or back, reminding myself that Facebook is just a dumb tool. Don't blame the tool. I decided to write a letter and send it to The Kid along with every other family member of legal age. My first draft was angry, so I toned it down and down again, nevertheless ending the letter with my disappointment and shame in discovering homophobia in the family, most of whom have known who I am for decades, but everyone? All the nephews? Did they know? I couldn't be sure because the subject of homosexuality had never come up with them explicitly.

But exterminating fags? Not acceptable.

I got a phone call from Sonny who was almost speechless with suppressed rage. How could I send a letter like that? Now The Kid wouldn't eat dinner and was convinced his family life was over. We talked, mostly right over one another's words. "This is the reason I'm not on Facebook," Sonny sobbed. "I don't want to know these things." She understood about my taking offense, but then she added, "You don't know until you've lived it."

"You don't know," she'd said, and I knew just what she meant: what it's like to be gay for example unless you, yourself are gay. Or are African–American. Or Muslim in America. I knew what she meant but did not buy it.

Tad's reactions went straight to the mattresses, as the saying goes. He had three things to tell me:
– "You are being intolerant and judgmental."
– "The boy doesn't have a problem. *You* have the problem."
– "If you're so upset, you ought to see a psychiatrist."

Someone at my nephew's school thought the lashing out on social media might have been a reaction to bullying, and another acquaintance suggested latent homosexuality and its accompanying shame as a possible explanation, but in the heat of the moment it is doubtful anyone in my family could have responded adequately to what I was feeling. What does it feel like to be called a fag by a relative who wishes all-God's-gay-children dead?

I remember staring at photos of The Kid taken at a younger age, then looking out the window as if the air itself were to blame. I still wonder if he will get over intolerance one day and come out the other side. Will I? Every gay person I know is, to a greater or lesser extent, in recovery from shame, striving not to live as victim but to rise above the anguish brought on by folks who might be well-intentioned but oblivious of the pain some words elicit. For that reason, I found myself conveying to people—to my family—emotions they didn't seem to grasp but needed to appreciate. I know this though: I will never have a child of my own, so part of my reaction centered on a hope of discovering in The Kid qualities akin to those I would have wanted to see in my own son.

*

Reflecting on that heartache once again during my current visit to Tad and Sonny's house, I meander outside and down the quarter-mile driveway of the property, which ends at a rural mailbox. There, I pivot to take in the cluster of farm buildings as sparks fly between my ears. Sparks associated with the present, sparks from the past. It's been six years since my father died. It has been two years since the Facebook incident.

I grew up with the people in this region of the country, friends and neighbors all believing something unique set us apart as not just decent folks but the best people in the world living in the best country on Earth. I still want to think those things are true despite enduring more than a decade of childhood and adolescent shame over being the person I am. In public school, I questioned values valued locally, including beliefs in arcane forces rather than logic, dogma rather than material cause and effect, sometimes a blatant disavowal of science and analytic understanding. The predominant local values I observed and rejected could be summarized in a few words: spiritualism, regionalism bordering on provincialism if not parochialism, denial, and conformity. Or stated more concretely: (1) faith in divine agency and the superiority of one's denomination, (2) distrust of most things urban strengthened by an affiliation with things rustic, (3) conviction that traditional ways are best, and (4) loyalty above all to one's family and the home team. I am disloyal under more than one of these tenets, worse, I am unsilent about being gay, thus at least part monster. But what is it, exactly, my relatives really think about my being a "fag?"

Lingering at the mailbox, I picture houses down the road and dotting intersecting lanes in the vicinity, each dwelling within the context of the larger neighborhood a community of the like-minded no less than applies back home along the crowded blocks of my city. Inside the houses in both locations folks prepare dinner, laugh, love, sometimes hate, and invariably act as humans. Here in mid-America, however, the occupants know their miles-distant neighbors in a personal way because many still live a stone's throw from their birthplace, and on any given day—every day—one hears only familiar dialects, shares comfortable views that rest on ungrounded foundations, trusts familiar flesh tones that are uniformly white, agrees on what is just and unjust, and reinforces local notions through repetition and nonstop breaking-news propaganda having little connection with realities of a complex world beyond. The local dynamic seems to involve an unlikely combination of honesty and naivety, honor and tunnel vision, virtue and repudiation.

When good people embrace curious philosophies, is it grounds for ridicule or tears? Is it possible to empathize while entirely rejecting another's viewpoint?

*

"So what's your favorite?"

"Hmm?"

"Your favorite meal for dinner."

I remind Sonny how much I like her meatloaf and garlic mashed potatoes—real country food—and that's what she fixes for us that evening. At one point during the meal, my last in this house for the year, Sonny says, "I wish you'd find somebody." How much can a person convey in five words? Worlds. I believe that had I asked her for fifty thousand dollars that night, Sonny would not have hesitated to jump in the car and drive to the local banker's house to pound his midnight door. *Wouldn't have battered an eye*, in Momspeak.

Which takes me back to that nonlinear fiction published in a literary review Tad had fluttered in the conversational breeze over breakfast sausages the first morning of my visit. That particular story had centered on violation and shame and loss, and never before had a product of my imagination elicited such mixed reactions from readers. One friend expressed rage over its characterization of Neanderthal behavior, whereas two others called me to say the ending made them cry. Both responses were gratifying because they confirmed at least a few people were moved by the message and had made the effort to say so. Which makes me wonder: what might it have been like if the souls who understand me now—today, as an adult living in urban America—had been present during my shame-filled growing years. What might happen today if The Kid enjoyed such compatriots, and if he appreciated my history and had a glimpse of my truth?

I try to formulate what, exactly, bothers me so much about the "death-to-fags" incident and how I'd like to see it resolved. I keep hearing my Mom's advice about holding one's tongue. A few years ago I read a three-part formula summarizing responses that might help repair a wrong. (1) Acknowledge the wrong, (2) apologize, and (3) atone in some way (unspecified) that feels appropriate. Good advice or not, it seems certain that ignoring what damaged a relationship is counterproductive to mending it.

*

Davenport, Iowa, and Minnetonka, Minnesota; faithful Sonny,

literal Tad, and their teenage son; my mother and father; Brunhilde Comstock and sweet Norm: I marvel at people and places and what they come to represent in a personal way. It's not that personalities and geographies framing a life are simply what they are; that idea short-suits causal complexities. Contemplating elements that underlie a life is a way of pointing back in time to one's history and ahead—along a tapestry of infinite textures illustrating what once was and what we still hope to experience or feel—between past mysteries and current expectations, all matters of interpretation.

In the foregoing snapshots from real life, the identities of people, physical locations, and family connections are camouflaged for the sake of protective decency, but the experiences and associated emotions have not been falsified. *As straight as a crow flies* is how my imperfect but exceptional mother would have put it.

We journey into a part of ourselves when revisiting old haunts, and in confronting a past that contours the present we might perceive irony where none is present, misfire in aspiring to cleverness, or misconstrue intent. We recall feelings of happiness and shame and hurt. We disengage in anger, or wait for a reason to forgive human failings beyond our ken. Saying what we think can cause hurt sometimes. Sometimes, what we don't or cannot say hurts most.

A Personal History of the "F" Word

The question I keep asking is how to account for the bitterness. Why are so many unwilling or unable to engage across the conservative–liberal divide? Why am I?

"We all did it as kids," my friend Sue reminds me over lunch, a shared Caesar salad with grilled chicken. We are both thinking back to days when we might have been guilty of fibbing, bullying, or being just plain "chicken" ourselves. A familiar exchange between children captures the idea:

"You're a big, fat scaredy-cat."

"I'm not scared."

"Yes, you are."

"No. *You* are."

"No, *you*."

We know the drill. Word-volley. But Sue shakes her head as we both wonder: does a deeper dynamic having to do with inverted truth lurk under the childish banter that could shed light on contemporary moral and political polarization? Take a more grown-up example of back-and-forth:

"You're all the same. More government and zero guns."

"No, you people want no government and zero regulation."

"Guns don't kill people, abortion kills people."

"More Americans have died from domestic bullets than in all our wars."

"Anyone can invent numbers."

What do these two conversations, childish versus arguably less childish, have in common? My lunch companion and I are talking about more than getting our conceptual nappies in a snit over a juvenile taunt, or over the mellifluous versus grating tone of voice of some right- or left-wing politician. We are discussing why so many citizens have declared interpersonal warfare triggered by deeply held—sometimes insupportable—opinion.

I tell Sue I just finished reading an essay by Ashraf H. A. Rushdy, "Reflections on Indexing My Lynching Book."[1] It details the widespread white justification for bloodlust directed against blacks over a century ago, reinforced by inventing or stretching facts to fit preconceived beliefs. Pro-lynching apologists often claimed an outrage, black beasts raping helpless white women, served as moral high ground for retaliation by noose justice. In reality, the history of slave ownership confirms the impunity with which white masters raped enslaved women, not vice versa, but to reinforce a strained logic, black women were blamed for inciting white masters to lust and rape. Granted, sexual baiting might have happened, but plain old racism was at work along with something else. Call it an unhealthy dose of justification or anxiety reduction, in this case pinning what whites had done around the necks of blacks, the very people upon whom violation had been visited.

During my teenage years, an uncle enjoyed "chewing the fat," as he put it, with my mother just before our evening meal at which he was a regular. Conversations turned cringe-worthy when he would bring up one of his pet topics, all those fat-a** boogies and lazy-a** jigaboos populating the rust-belt city in which he worked as a factory security guard during graveyard shift. I remember wondering at the time how my exceptional black teacher in grade school might have responded to this relative as he vented to Mom, but kids of the era in my household were to be seen and not heard. Years later, with tongue untied, I asked another family member to stop using the "N" word in my house. When he resurrected the issue one holiday, he seemed on the verge of apologizing.

"You don't understand what I mean when I use that word."

I felt cheered. Until he explained.

"What I mean is really stupid people."

In an environment of self-deception to justify demeaning epithets, it's not surprising that a while later, a fifteen-year-old member of the clan posted his desire on the Internet to burn "retarded" feminists at the stake and rid the world of fags. When I despaired to family members of the misogyny and homophobia underlying those youthful yearnings, more than one relative rallied to the boy's defense by stating he held ill will toward nobody; rather, I was the one being intolerant. A good boy did not have a problem. I had the problem.

The neurologist Henry Head long ago differentiated between two types of sensations or feelings. Epicritic experiences are fine and localized discriminations of touch or pain. Protopathic sensibility is poorly localized, more visceral or emotional and can be paroxysmal. My reaction to a relative's use of the "F" word was protopathic, deep and enduring.

In retrospect, part of the difficulty seems to have centered on my choice of words. By invoking the label, "homophobia," I'd hoped to elicit familial understanding or empathy for reasons having to do with my personal identity. Instead, the term was perceived as name-calling and interpreted as a declaration of war. How to explain the 180-degree reversal, with me in the perceived role of heterophobe?

As a neurophysiologist by training, I am not an enthusiast of psychoanalytic theories, whereas my friend Sue, a practicing psychiatrist, is more familiar with the territory. Both of us agree it is too easy to clobber people with high-toned diagnoses and alienate them; nevertheless, we both credit insights in the realm of unconscious coping techniques to ward off anxiety.[2] Do the ideas have relevance to current polarizations of opinion much in the news? Here is a proposition worth considering: at least one of five anxiety-reducing strategies can underlie inverted-truth propositions, which I will dub the "I'm-OK-But-You're-Not" dynamic. The mechanisms include (1) denial, (2) projection, (3) splitting, (4) rationalization, and (5) disgust- and fear-based illogic. Others could be added to the list, but these five earn top billing in my book.

In the aforementioned fraidy-cat dialogue and its variants, an accused child might refuse to admit fear because the kid is not fearful. But if fear is felt, shame might rear its unwelcome head. Rather than confess to an anxiety-inducing emotion that weakens one's self image and identity reflected in the eyes of another—rather than acknowledge shame—the child refutes having the emotion of fear. This is the home turf of denial, sometimes described by psychologists as "primitive" because it is often expressed during childhood as a refusal to accept reality.

In contrast to reflected identity, people sometimes actively project an identity onto another. Projection, the second mechanism in the list, involves incorrectly attributing one's unwelcome thoughts or feelings onto someone else, especially when the thoughts or feelings are anathema. As a follow-on to denial in the fraidy-cat exchange, the child projects fear onto another person. In this case, the I'm-OK-But-You're-Not response is basic stuff that comes naturally. Kids don't think much about how they react, but what about adults when it comes to moral or political opinion?

The role of projection in historic black lynchings seems obvious today, but discernment is not always evident in the heat of the moment. When I asked an adult relative my own age to consider the idea that he might be engaged in a denial of bigotry regarding the feminazi/fag comments posted by a teenage kid on Facebook, his response was also perhaps predictable. He denied being in denial, adding I was the one guilty of being "judgmental and intolerant." More projection.

Splitting, a third coping mechanism, is as commonplace as projection but in some respects more interesting. It was difficult during his presidency to avoid encountering statements claiming Donald Trump was the devil incarnate or a national hero. Add to the list Barack Obama, Ronald Reagan, Gloria Steinem, Justin Bieber, the Pope, Hillary Clinton, and dozens of others in or out of the news, and the story is similar. An individual espousing intense feelings might generalize an indictment or praise, depending on political party and other alignments, to all liberals or conservatives, or to all religious advocates or atheists, or to all young pop stars. In the realm of black-and-white thinking, of clown journalism and kneejerk partisanship à la Fox News and MSNBC, scant middle ground is in sight; we and everyone who thinks as we think are right, whereas they and everyone like them are wrong. Why reason on the basis of an individual's worthiness or faults—or the logical merit of a given position—when it feels better to indict an entire group, all African Americans for example, all Republicans or Muslims, all who are welfare recipients, or drug addicts or terrorists or jihadists or something-else-ists? This is the home turf of the splitting landscape in which extreme polarization or splitting of opinion into good and evil is the pathway to veracity, to hell with middle ground because there is none, and hello Truth, because I am the one who owns it even if I distort or invert it.

Such thinking is nothing new even in intellectual circles. During the early twentieth century, scholars rallied to one side or the other of the nature–nurture controversy. Are we what and who we are because of biology or the environment? Although the debate simmers today, the Canadian psychologist, Donald Hebb,[3] convincingly argued from data a more modern view that we are a product of both nature and nurture, up to 100% owing to genetics and 100% to our surroundings. It's akin to asking whether length or width is more important to determine the area of a rectangle, Hebb offered. Is a given U.S. President a demon or angel then, and how about that intemperate uncle of mine? Might the two individuals contain a bit of both good and bad?

Rationalization, a fourth coping mechanism in the list, involves distorting facts until thinking makes the distortion appear to represent reality. Think of rationalization as unconscious self-deception to reduce psychological discomfort through justifications that seem plausible but are not, in reality, legitimate. In the realm of not-rational rationalization, something approaching genuine empathy might be reduced to false do-goodism. Why donate money to feed the poor if all those losers will just buy more drugs, for example.

Rationalizations abound in political campaigns and shroud many hot topics. When shown reliable, statistical data on gun violence in the U.S., an acquaintance of mine dismissed the numbers by responding, "Anyone can say anything. Everybody is biased these days." This is an example of wanting to win an argument so much that anything goes, including carpet-bombing with words just to win. Unwelcome hard evidence, cause and effect, and intellectual or academic authority might be viewed as desirable or undesirable, depending on one's outlook and willingness to reason, but they can also be dismissed as their opposites, namely untrustworthy, elitist, or proof of what this same acquaintance calls intellectual bigotry. When asked to read about splitting, this person stated that no such thing existed. "I don't need to read articles or books," he maintained, "besides, history doesn't mean anything anymore because it's just someone's opinion, no better than my own." Such abjuration is a remarkable combination of several unconscious defense mechanisms, with rationalization stage center.

Theory suggests that the strategies of denial, projection, splitting, and rationalization are unconscious, but most of us are at least partly aware of moral or political dilemmas and our reactions to them. The idea of cognitive dissonance[4] addresses conscious conflicts and the discomfort or tension arising from conflicting attitudes and beliefs. Even an ardent pro-choice advocate, if sane, does not condone the wholesale taking of human life, so how can the conflict of life-taking via abortion be justified? One option is to define the beginning of "life" in a way that is acceptable, if at odds with pro-life definitions. Another way to reduce the conflict is to argue that abortion is a medical decision between physician and patient, thus politicians should keep laws from female bodies. The flip side of cognitive dissonance is cognitive consonance: we seek out what makes us feel more harmonious with the world and ourselves. When listening to an emotionally charged discussion about abortion for example, we might focus on what strengthens our viewpoint and helps us feel better. To the extent that we want to support our position or beliefs, we attend to and incorporate information bolstering our personal position and may not even be aware that we are not processing counter arguments.

To the four coping mechanisms discussed so far, I would add a fifth response pertinent to political or moral polarization. Fear-based illogic is a horse of a different temperament. We hear its echoes all the time: guns don't kill people; people kill people. Though many individuals might acknowledge the proposition somehow "feels" right or wrong, it's difficult to put a finger on the exact reason. However, the notion that "guns are never the problem, but people are always the problem" is black-and-white thinking already characterized as splitting.

Another way to look at the NRA's assertion that guns don't kill people is to consider the missing elements: let's say the proposition is true for the sake of argument, but then what should be done about guns, if anything? This is a complex issue because several mechanisms are at work, as is the case in most controversies. Taken at face value, the statement "Guns don't kill people" is empirically false. Guns kill more than 80 people a day in the U.S. on average (including suicides, though estimated numbers are just that), so a more accurate mantra might be that guns do kill people, and people with guns kill people. However, what a gun advocate usually means is that guns properly disabled and safely locked away do not kill people by themselves. Besides, automobiles kill as many folks as guns do, more or less. A counter argument is that autos are not designed explicitly to kill or maim, and guns are impulse accelerators. To the comeback that cars, too, can function as impulse accelerators, one could answer that all cars and drivers are licensed regularly. Arguments might continue endlessly, but it is doubtful opposing sides can reconcile when one camp remains fiercely motivated by an underlying fear that big, corrupt government will confiscate firearms along with other "Constitutionally guaranteed rights" and the opposing camp fears and deplores everything to do with instruments designed to shoot bullets.

Brain research is beginning to provide insights into neurophysiological mechanisms underlying personal and political ideology. We frequently hear that a powerful, causal factor behind hatred is fear. Let me say that again: fear can result in hatred. One might then wonder what could trigger fear or accompany it with respect to belief systems or dogma. Could the basic and universal emotion of disgust have anything to do with one's political ideology or moral perceptions?

One of the earliest scientific studies on disgust is included in Darwin's

The Expression of the Emotions in Man and Animals.[5] The emotion of disgust is roughly defined in psychology these days as a feeling of revulsion or intense displeasure to something unpleasant or offensive. As with pornography, we know it when we see it. However, to be rigorous and reproducible, contemporary scientific studies variously define human disgust in terms of "disgust sensitivity" measured on standardized surveys or questionnaires to emotionally evocative images, such as those in the International Affective Picture System (IAPS) database.

Inbar, Pizarro, and Bloom[6] have suggested that an individual's general predisposition to feelings of disgust can play an important role in one's social life. Results from two studies by these researchers showed that proneness to disgust was associated (that is, statistically correlated) with greater self-reported political conservatism, and the linkage is strongest for issues centered on purity, such as attitudes toward homosexuality. Terrizini, Shook, and Ventis[7] supported the positive correlation and added that inducing disgust increases prejudicial attitudes for conservatives and reduces prejudice for liberals.

Such correlational reports are suggestive, but how and where does something like revulsion operate in the human brain when it comes to social or political values? P. Read Montague[8] and ten coworkers from Virginia Tech and elsewhere attempt to answer this question by measuring human brain responses directly with functional magnetic resonance imaging (fMRI).

While 41 male and 42 female test subjects (ages 18 to 62) were monitored in an fMRI scanner, they viewed pictures that included disgusting, threatening, pleasant, and neutral images and then rated all the pictures they had seen. Afterward, participants completed questionnaires about their political attitudes and sensitivity to disgust. Brain responses to a disgusting picture were enough to predict an individual's political orientation. This was true even when a person's verbal rating of images (reports of low disgust for example) disagreed with the brain's reaction (strong neural activation response). Details from this experiment were remarkable: brain-based prediction of a person's liberal or conservative views was accurate 95% of the time on the basis of a single disgusting image, with conservatives biased toward the negative, that is, showing a stronger disgust and threat response in brain areas such as prefrontal and insulary cortex and the amygdala, which is involved in supporting memory for emotionally arousing experiences, including anxiety. (My friend Sue tells me as an aside from her clinical practice that lowering electrical activity in the subcortical amygdala with promising computer-based treatments might be a way of reducing post-traumatic stress disorder with greater success than previous approaches, such as medication.)

Political ideology—including attitudes about family, sex, education, and personal autonomy—is now being shown to reflect, at least in part, basic biological mechanisms that help defend against perceptions such as physical threat. People like to think their political opinions are objective or at least rational, but the study by Montague and his coworkers strongly suggests emotions play a greater role than previously thought, and that role might lie outside our awareness or gainsay verbal statements. The head (mouth) says one thing, but the heart (or in this case, emotional brain) begs another.

A disconnect between what humans feel (experience internally) versus express (say or do) may not be too surprising in view of the fact that many animals defend against physical threat through the well-known fight-or-flight response. A rabbit that does not flee may still be threatened or terrified. It is tempting to speculate on a possible interplay between disgust and shame in humans: if the brain responds with disgust (say, in a racial context) but the public voice says "no, I harbor no prejudicial feelings," might the overt expression have something to do with shame-induced denial, just as a child might deny fear because of shame?

Neuropsychologists like to talk about our brain's internally generated version of reality, which may not always agree with the world "out there." An internal model—as it is called—of experience or memory is a way of organizing and representing what we perceive, so that our interpretation of "reality" depends on our experiences along with cultural biases and related factors. This idea is often discussed in the context of vision, where visual parts of the brain can process more information than the eyes send in. The world, for instance, remains steady in terms of our perception even though our eyes dart around. Perceptions are not straightforward reproductions of data from the eye to brain but are reconstructions in the brain shaped by expectations, probability, and memory.[9] But what about morality? If an internal model evokes disgust in the context of, for example, homosexuality, would that inner model not shape one's moral and political opinion regardless of what one says?

Data from fMRI alone may not completely explain what's behind the polarizing I'm-OK-But-You're-Not stance, but such information points the way to clearer understanding of what's going on at the neuronal level. Because of educational bias, I favor a physiological approach as potentially the most productive whereas Sue combines that avenue with psychodynamics, placing equal emphasis on mental and emotional processes that may be unconscious and shaped by early childhood experiences. Sue is more optimistic than I am as well, possibly because her professional commitment—treating vets returning to Fort Knox from conflict and trauma—is centered on real-world experience plus an expectation that injured brains and bodies can be mended, or at least modified for improved adaptability to a tough world. Even she has dark moments however when caseloads diminish her role to pill pimping and she reflects on how government funding agencies erratically address struggling veterans.

Like many others of my generation, I left the overcast Midwest in search of brighter skies and outlooks, settling decades ago along the West Coast where residents do not complain quite so much about weather mucking up a metaphorical climate of shame and disgust. Here at home, minority neighbors are visible everywhere and often are, like myself, transplants. Looking back several decades, it's tempting to remember the pleasant and discount the disagreeable, leaving me slightly nostalgic, yet largely disenthralled, about the past. My parents quibbled about politics, but they remained respectful while favoring either the political party of the "little guy" (Mom) or no-nonsense "business interests" (Dad), and they voted during every election, unlike many Americans today. A mental reboot of yesteryear reminds me most families in our sphere back then did not engage in emotional battles over irreconcilable viewpoints at the evening meal. These days, many of my extended family and I are at opposite ends of the spectrum in ways I would never have anticipated.

What do I mean by a climate of shame and disgust back on the home front? First, the disgust. When I do return for a visit to the place of my adolescence, semi-rural mid-America, it is tempting to pass judgment on local values through which residents often claim moral high ground while looking down at outsiders, such as city slickers, feminists, gays, minorities, welfare moms, and all those immigrants. In doing so, self-righteousness becomes apparent, generalizations abound, and insulting epithets are common. But that is a two-way street. For example, it seems to me that almost every household where I grew up remains a community of the like-minded, and that is also true in my current urban neighborhood of largely mixed-ethnic, liberal, whale huggers who are happy to ridicule hicks frittering their lives away in corn country. In both places one sees a predisposition to smugness and towering self-righteousness, but there is a difference.

In households rooted in the turf of my adolescence, one sees faces of only pale flesh tones, hears words with reinforcing overtones in only one language, witnesses expressions of faith over fact in propositions that stand on wobbly but unchallenged legs. Most of my relatives still live within a cultural cocoon only a stone's throw from the houses in which they were born. They live and love miles—light years, really—from me geographically and disconnected from my way of thinking, tuned always to a single channel of information with little possibility of real news about an incredibly diverse world—where, yes indeed, the climate is changing—reaching out occasionally but never absorbing in a personal way much to do with that world, keeping a firm hold on entrenched beliefs and values, innocence and naivety, loyalty and purity. And if that is so—at least the innocence and purity parts—is it tragedy or cause for rejoicing?

Jonathon Haidt,[10] a social psychologist from NYU, suggests that a liberal-minded person tends to be more open to new experiences than a conservative person; however, five or six moral values or systems form the core of political choices whether an individual identifies as left, right, or center. A liberal-minded person tends to honor two of the values most: minimizing harm while maximizing care (think Hippocratic Oath), and fairness/reciprocity (in essence, adhering to the Golden Rule). Conservatives honor those two values highly as well, but they also nurture three additional roots of morality: ingroup *loyalty* (faithfulness to their own kind), *respect* for authority (for example, police or church), and *purity* of mind and body (for example, abortion is murder). Liberals care little about these three concepts and sometimes reject them. A proposed connection between political conservatism and the idea of purity is reminiscent of findings from the Inbar study and others.

I worry that some explanations suggested by experts are too facile to address the complex factors underlying political, moral, and religious opinion. Is a single dynamic at work in a given situation or a dozen? Do we understand any of them fully, to say nothing about our beginner's concept of brain wiring? And isn't branding a person either liberal or conservative—racist or not—far too simplistic? Sue and I add another wrinkle to the quandary by asking an uncomfortable question.

"Could racism have some basis in biology, which is to say, evolution?"

The suggestion feels unnerving, even sinister, as though we are imagining a justification for eugenics or worse. I like to regard myself as nonracist, but can anyone claim to be entirely without thoughts of cultural bias, no matter one's skin color? I have to work on occasion at consciously suppressing negative judgment of others of a different culture or nationality or color. Doesn't everyone? Do such thoughts qualify as racism, and if so, is the tendency biological or entirely cultural (learned)? The evolutionary speculation Sue and I are mulling is that, as humans evolved, it might have become biologically adaptive for survival purposes to favor and protect our kind, that is "us," and to distrust unfamiliar or foreign hunter-gatherers, "them," especially given competition for resources. Such conjecture flies in the face of social–scientific dogma holding that differences among human societies are cultural and not genetic, to say nothing of the contemporary biological viewpoint that "race" is an unscientific term.[11,12] But even if the idea of some biological basis for racist behavior (such as bigotry) turns out to have validity, it is grounds for contemporary discrimination no more than a presumptive instinct for human aggression justifies torture or genocide. Furthermore, the hypothesis of biologically based racism would operate as a two-way street, favoring no particular "master" race or country over another in a civilized world. These are swampy waters, but they illustrate the emotional burden and complexity inherent in trying to unravel the origin of social judgments made by humans.

When I taught neuropsychology, I cautioned students against the error of hypostatization. To put it simply, explaining something merely by giving it a name is often no explanation at all. ("Of course she's homeless; she's crazy." "The kid's a thief because he's delinquent.") Labels are fine so long as they are linked to a deeper understanding of—and explanation for—a given behavior together with the possibility of prediction and control of that behavior. However, when bandied about injudiciously, a tag can induce counterproductive responses, including hostility, as happened when accusing my family of homophobia.

Finally, about that climate of shame back in corn country. In reflecting on my extended family, I believe our hearts beat as one in hopes for common ground fertile in common sense, but in areas of morality and politics, otherwise decent people intending no harm can be utterly irrational. I know I am.

My father did not give voice to sexual matters except on one occasion when I was in middle school. In a moment of breathtaking humiliation for me, he issued in earnest tones a warning about guarding against perverted men. I knew at once, though he did not, that I was the gay person my father was warning me against.

Because I'm a homosexual male who grew up in rural America in an era of police harassment and gay bashings and Stonewall riots, the word "fag" is a blasting cap still detonating in my brain. The pejorative is a reminder of shame, whether uttered in irony today by a gay acquaintance in San Francisco or with loathing by an unwitting kid or a Gospel-brandishing believer from the Bible Belt. When I re-evaluate whether neighbors or relatives discount bigotry or I overreact to the "F" word, I remind myself of denial, projection, splitting, rationalization, and complex fear- and threat-based mechanisms capable of inverting truth but also serving as splendid coping mechanisms for individuals struggling to make it through the day. I reflect on our emotional brain about which we often have little insight, then on the generous mantle of gray matter that makes us social mammals of intellect, both more and less, for better or worse.

The humane socialist economist E. F. Schumacher cautioned that the proper work for us in curing contemporary problems is to work on ourselves, not to take the either–or approach but one *and* the other.[13] Understanding oneself and others often resides in the vicinity of middle ground, in the idea of balance—often the higher ground—in both discourse and in our heads. Although knowing that much will solve neither the world's problems nor my own, it might help in negotiating the conservative–liberal divide with greater civility.

Left or Right: The Fear Factor

Americans who survived the Vietnam War era (1961–75) recall living with anxiety. Students feared the draft and dodging bullets in some foreign jungle. Parents were terrified by the prospect of losing a son. Politicians warned of the global erosion of democracy from a Communist-led domino effect. Those in the military were vilified, and some were abandoned after returning to a country that no longer felt like home to them. Many voters were outraged by a deceitful White House, while others deplored the depraved antics of counterculture hippies. Women, African Americans, farmworkers, and minorities charged the "system" with ongoing oppression. During those turbulent years, most people, regardless of political persuasion, believed that on many levels of experience—personally, culturally, politically, nationally—the U.S. was in serious trouble.

Approximately 80% of Americans and citizens of other nations who are alive today are too young to remember much about the Vietnam War. I thought back then I would never live through more anxious and disturbing times. I was mistaken.

On first encountering the expression "identity politics," I didn't know what it meant. Reflecting on the way people I know react to the news these days however, I realize many of us have become single-issue voters. Some of my social-media friends have "unfriended" one another because of political opinions, or they edit what they say. An acquaintance divorced her husband after the 2016 election because of serious arguments about politics. Aunts or uncles are no longer welcome at holiday gatherings. Disagreements arise at the mere mention of abortion, guns, gangs, arming teachers, political correctness, black lives, blue lives, economic inequality, immigration, evolution, viruses, nuclear brinksmanship, and climate change. Of late, initiating a conversation can feel like stepping into a minefield in a land of magical thinking.

Identity politics refers to individuals making decisions according to social categories or ideologies that are often political. Examples are women supporting feminist causes and gays voting for LGBTQ rights. Two overarching and often mutually excluding identities today are liberal versus conservative, or left versus right. We constantly hear about irreconcilable differences in Washington, D.C.; indeed, we can hardly escape the thunder in an era of lightning mass media, and the racket is usually about "them," those other guys on the wrong side of an issue, and us.

I would like to propose a more unifying idea, the concept that folks on the left and right—even extreme ideologues who steadfastly adhere to some political stance—have more in common with antagonists than they might suppose. Indeed, we are all acting much the same way for a reason.

In what follows, it is relevant to clarify than my background is in physiology and psychology with a focus on the structure and function of the brain. That context is germane (though my political opinions are not) because one interpretation of what's happening now in the U.S.— and to some extent elsewhere—centers on the human brain with its unique trick of discovering its own existence, yet sometimes ignoring pertinent information. Nothing else in the known universe can pull off such feats: self-discovery plus a voluntary disavowal of what might readily be acknowledged as fact. Put another way, the human brain is adept at conjuring distorted notions, some of which can be delusional. A more common mental departure from reality is denial, one of several defense mechanisms for rejecting what is right before our eyes. Are we all delusional then, in denial, or is something more basic going on?

Here's a peek at how the brain can sometimes work using an example—much in the news for several years—of Donald Trump lovers versus haters. Trump is one person, and everybody can observe what he says, does, and how he says and does it, but judgments about the man could not be more divergent. The more Donald misbehaves, in the opinion of Trump haters, the more the Donald-lovers like him. How is it possible? Are people in the opposite camps even living in the same mental universe?

"I don't disagree with a single thing the President did in office," a female acquaintance said recently. She is a decent woman who can be counted on in times of difficulty. "What's wrong with people anyway?" she asks. "Don't they want to make America great again?"

Let's consider the statements in more detail. In what follows, I acknowledge the essay by Thomas Singer entitled, "Trump and the American Collective Psyche."[14] His is an analysis worth reading, but the content is quite technical and difficult unless a reader is familiar with psychiatric terminology. Here's a more accessible and modified analysis.

What I think the Trump supporter is really asking is not, "Don't you want to make American great again?" Rather she is pleading, "Don't you want *me* to feel great again? Because I am not great right now. In fact, I feel injured and broken. I feel a loss of my sense of place in my own country. And the person you detest so much, Trump, has been our best hope for a fix, my fix, because he understands my injury and says out loud what I'm feeling."

This woman's adoration is reinforced by a hope of restoration through a single male. Criticism of her hero threatens her certainty and rapture, much like a religious individual encountering a crisis of faith and fearful of falling from grace.

Charged feelings are equally evident in the expressions of her NRA-loving mate. He likes a loud motorcycle vibrating against his loins, and it's tempting to joke about his Harley as a phallic symbol, but the guns in his collection are more than symbolic. He loves his guns and shooting them, but why? It isn't merely that he adores guns as adult toys or suffers from penis envy. Attack his gun, and you attack him. Protest against guns in the street and you are not protesting for the safety of school children, you are not marching against the NRA in his mind; you are attacking all guns, our national gun heritage in the Land of the Free, and, in particular, his personal guns. You are attacking *him*. Deprive him of a gun—even one gun in a vast collection—and you take away his best friend, his security, and his identity. In one sense, he *is* his gun. That's identity politics with a polarizing recoil.

My Trump- and gun-loving acquaintances are patriotic citizens, and they cheer when America wins at something, but their overriding concerns, evident on Facebook posts and in conversations, have to do with feeling aggrieved amid chaos. Job security and family income have been threatened in recent years. They feel burdened by soaring healthcare costs while at the same time providing financial support for unemployed offspring who continue to bring into the world new mouths to feed. Accompanying the loss of personal solvency and pride and identity within a country they once knew and felt they understood is a sense of entitlement to better treatment. Top it off with a pandemic, and their sense of personal security has taken a catastrophic hit.

A fundamental factor shaping their politics and everyday lives has to do with fear. Fear of government interference in their lives and wallets. Fear of thugs and immigrants and cheaters stealing their benefits and tax dollars. Fear of most things liberals stand for, just as progressives fear some of the very things conservatives champion. When they talk about their views on abortion or assault weapons, my acquaintances are really speaking about themselves, and they tend to overlook what they do not want to consider, as all of us do.

Thinking back to what happened to us as a nation during the Vietnam War era, I suggest parallel reactions are occurring now. The same types of emotion are being expressed by people on the right and left. I am not proposing liberals who champion Joe Biden or Kamala Harris believe in the principles and solutions conservatives value, rather that the brains of liberals and conservatives are up to the same, old tricks that have been evident for millennia, and a self-defensive cloaking device in the noggin is covering its tracks.

If you're a naturalist or biologist or some other brand of scientist, and you observe the Earth being degraded, and you appreciate planetary and climate balance are essential to life as we know it, then you likely feel a sense of personal injury and urgency these days. If you're a conservative, and you picture an unborn baby being aborted, and life is sacrosanct according to your definition of life, then you feel grief or personal injury. If you're a feminist and you hear an elected male is accused of sexual harassment or rape and brags about it, you judge the politician to be a creep to be feared. If you're an unemployed coal miner in Appalachia and you are losing your house and your kid just died from a drug overdose, what does it matter if some Arctic ice melts or freezes over, but it's comforting to hear the suggestion that melting is a hoax anyway. Job loss to globalization and automation, racial bias, downward mobility, discrimination on the basis of sex or sexual preference: it doesn't matter so much whether you identify politically as red or blue when you are hurting or overwhelmed by a sense of hopelessness. Though the triggers and details differ among individuals, you are feeling the same thing as the other guy. You are experiencing injury or helplessness. One way to counteract helplessness—though it might seem counterintuitive—is to identify with a bully, just as domestic abuse victims sometimes stand by their abusive partner in public.

Injury is scary inside our heads, and a central factor underlying most political hot topics these days is anxiety, as it was during Vietnam. It's an old saw in psychology that fear and anger are strongly linked. In physiological terms, both emotions involve arousal of the central nervous system (brain and spinal cord) in response to a threat. Accelerated heart rate and breathing, sweating, tremor, narrowed vision, and a host of other responses are triggered when the drug adrenalin (epinephrine) activates the brain. Over the longer term, we can experience paranoia, black-and-white thinking, isolation, panic attacks, and low levels of testosterone and oxytocin. The latter is a neurotransmitter now thought to enhance pro-social feelings of empathy and trust especially towards ingroup members, but to enhance aggressive feelings toward the outgroup.

When confronted by injury or its likelihood, our brain communicates, "Wake up and watch out!" because responding to a threat is imperative to life itself. People can respond with fear or anger, which can lead to rage and hate, or fear can activate defense mechanisms that obscure the recognition of reality. Anger is also a wired-in behavior that can help mask a person's fear. For example, anger can defend a person against feeling hurt and out of control, or against grief, and it can mask inner tension or a desire for empowerment.

If you're a rabbit in a hay field and you're confronted by a threat, you have few options: freeze in place, fight, or flee. Rabbits flee or freeze on the spot because they are lousy fighters. If you're a human being facing a threat, you can opt to do nothing at all or fight or run away as well, but ancient parts of the human brain (called the limbic system) provide other options centering on emotion. The amygdala in particular helps to regulate fear.[15] We can internalize the fear we feel. We can get mad. We can externalize blame and hate others, and we often do just that. A cold and clammy reaction, especially the freezing-in-place variety, is one expression of paralyzing fear. Hot anger is the fight part of the fight-or-flight response to threat, especially when a person is emotionally invested in a belief or, worse, thinks a gun is the solution.

The idea that the same brain mechanisms are operating in folks on the political left and right (even though triggers for threats and external manifestations of fear and anger might be quite different) can be summarized in three steps.

1.   The first step involves a cause or trigger. We feel threatened or injured or emotionally wounded about something personally meaningful. Think job loss, bankruptcy, deportation, a killer virus, or your child being shot dead in the street or in school.

2. The second step is a physiological mechanism. The body shoots adrenalin everywhere, and by the time adrenalin and other neurotransmitters get to the brain and are experienced as emotion, a threat or injury manifests as fear or anger, which can lead to hate.

3. The third step is a solution. We seek relief from emotional injury, as we would for a physical wound. Quick relief might come through split-second decisions, or we might make premature conclusions involving black-and-white thinking, unjustifiably separating what we believe to be good from bad, friend from enemy. In the end, the reaction is consolidated into a belief reinforced through selective attention. From there on, we can respond without the need to think things through.

What constitutes a threat or potential source of injury to you? The answer, much like triggers for political polarization, depends on many factors. For example, if you form opinions from watching only MSNBC or Fox News on television, your knowledge base will be quite different from that of someone who reads lots of respected and refereed science journals. If the news you watch on TV serves up threats to consolidate a particular response or reinforce paranoia, your idea of what even constitutes a threat will be shaped accordingly.

Let's take the specific case of abortion. Is abortion a threat in your opinion, equivalent to murder, or is it a basic human right? Your viewpoint likely depends on whether you are a devout Christian fundamentalist or a hands-off-my-body women's libber. If your philosophy or religion holds that conscious life (and susceptibility to murder) begins with conception (fertilization of egg with sperm), your idea of abortion as an assault on life would differ markedly from that of most biologists. But when, really, does the awareness associated with human life begin, and with it, the full complement of human rights? We use words such as consciousness, awareness, and attention as if we know what they mean, but even psychologists who study the concepts for a living acknowledge the age-old and present-day difficulties inherent in understanding these complicated topics. Nevertheless, if you define your personhood and identity as championing the unborn, then your political identity is almost certainly Republican these days regardless of whether the party leader is saint or sinner, savior or bigot. You see the mercy in your stance and tend to overlook the rest. As psychologists express it, you maintain cognitive consonance or an internal consistency of thought compatible with your beliefs. A related concept is confirmation bias: looking at any new evidence as if it confirms existing views. The trouble is that only attending to what we already suspect is true means we also ignore or remain impervious to what is *objectively* true, in other words, reality.

Is a stable world climate a human right and in your thoughts a lot these days? Again, the answer depends on whether you are a tree hugger or lumberjack. Was Trump as President a fierce protector of the nation or racist scum? A white Christian fundamentalist and Muslim refugee would likely answer differently.

Given a perceived threat, where is relief to be found? For a person with progressive views, relief might come through political activism or regulation, such as protesting guns or marching for social justice. As a conservative, relief might be channeled through a leader who verbalizes the things you feel down deep inside but are not supposed to say, someone who tells you illegals are criminals and responsible for taking your job, and all those welfare cheats are robbing you blind. Relief might come from a man who jokes glaciers are not shrinking and winters are colder these days, and the whole business of global warming is fake, a leader who talks about bringing back law and order, improving economic conditions, and restoring national glory. If you are a Biden liberal and reflect on Donald Trump, what you see is a manipulator, serial liar, science-denier, and admitted pussy grabber, and relief comes from disavowing him as a leader and maybe supporting incarceration. If you are a scientist who has dedicated a career to studying the natural world, then climate change threatens the things you care about, and relief comes from addressing global warming through prompt and science-validated action. To the scientist in you, an important part of your identity, Trump was an intellectually barren, morally bankrupt, politically toxic, and mentally ill science denier.

The key here is to appreciate, whether Republican or Democrat, left or right, hawk or dove, red or blue—that is, regardless of identity politics—you are responding much the same way your perceived antagonist responds. You behave according to the way the human brain has functioned since cavemen huddled around fires or responded to the perception or reality of injury. When you feel threatened or wounded, the injury elicits fear or anger, and what you require is relief from the cause of injury. In other words, regardless of personal or political opinions, we all respond with predictable reactions and emotions orchestrated by the brain. The difference between a person on the left or right originates from the trigger, that is, the cause of perceived injury. If you appreciate why the trigger is a spark for someone's fear or anger, you can better understand why the individual supports a position or person that brings relief even when that solution might be your own personal trigger for injury.

A friend of mine recently posted on the Internet, "I just don't get U.S. gun culture. It's totally wacko." Indeed, gun culture appears to be bizarre if you are the kind of person who feels threatened by guns. Then the threat of injury to others or yourself from a gun triggers anxiety, and the relief you require resides in stricter gun laws. But if you feel threatened by gangs rather than guns, or by an intrusive and untrusted government, or by an antagonist who wants to outlaw guns, then buying a bigger gun for self-defense is just the ticket to address your anxiety and quell it. In each case, the organ inside the skull is operating according to the principle of self-preservation.

Apply the same reasoning to other hot-button issues, from building or removing a border wall to eliminating or increasing food stamps for hungry children, and what seems wacko on the surface becomes understandable. The brain is simply doing its job.

The real picture of course is far more complex than the simple model presented here. Neuropsychology is complicated: there aren't just a couple of neurotransmitters in the brain but interactions among potentially several dozen, and it isn't only the amygdala that plays a role but exquisitely complex brain circuitry involving many centers and millions of neurons. Culture and genetics matter, as do education along with recent and early-childhood experiences. A simple model of threat-derived fear and anger does not address extreme behaviors, ranging from antisocial pathology or malignant narcissism to violent expressions of hatred. Clearly, there are extremists and fools out there, but the next time your aunt or grandpa fumes about some topic in a seemingly irrational way, think about the central nervous system we all share in common and a brain that wants, above all, to be safe.

God, Sex, and War to a Triple-A Alien

At the most fundamental level of human inquiry, the quantum level, physics tells us causation is a blur. An insistence on poor focus is hardly good news for empiricists who like to think about identifiable causes and effects, but it's not that effects aren't caused, exactly. Rather, science in all its contemporary sophistication can't pin down the where-ness and when-ness of elemental (really tiny) events because they are regulated by non-concrete and unintuitive agencies operating in space–time. The best we can do in trying to specify causation is to say something about probability. Nature then, functions a bit like a giant casino in setting the odds. Uncertainty may be anathema to non-gamblers and confusing to almost everybody else because ambiguity muddles our common-sense concept of reality.

We think reality is just real. Something is real or it isn't real, true or not true: end of story. So what is real, and what is true? We think we know, but is time real in the same sense that a rock or an antelope is real? Is light a wave behaving something like the surface of an ocean, or is it a train of fast-moving photons? Science says light is both, a wave and not-wave. Because of such difficulties, the better business of inquiry, according to both physicists and philosophers who study such matters these days, is to look not for causes—that is, not to the underlying nature of stuff according to its predecessors—but to think in terms of laws by which phenomena operate in the here and now. Laws might be less blurry than causes and perhaps more revealing.

Given the ambiguities attendant on cause and effect, reality and unreality, what are some laws to help us understand ourselves, for instance, how individuals think and function as human beings in a complex world? Because we have to start somewhere, let's consider the way people think about three nearly universal aspects of life: religion, sexuality, and war. Practically everybody has a personal viewpoint about God, sex, and bullets, but the topics can be of particular interest to nonconforming individuals.

As a religious nonbeliever, a sexual outsider, and a military antagonist and detractor, I am thrice alien to the values embraced by a good portion of my countrymen, including many friends and family members. For a triple-A-rated human alien like myself—an A-theist, A-hetero, A-military sort of person—are there any laws that might help explain my minority views to a skeptical and often disapproving majority? There are such laws.

Religion

Claims about the glories and villainies associated with religion are so pervasive these days, and so emotionally laden, that lots of folks have hunkered or bunkered themselves down into a sort of peevish mental-emotional withdrawal from those who would politicize or evangelize. In unemotional terms, it can be argued that one of the principal findings from science is that the world—indeed everything in it and the universe itself insofar as anyone can comprehend such a concept—is determined by and interpretable according to rational laws rather than through ghosts (holy or otherwise), magical thinking, mystical propositions, spiritual and emotional claims, or nonempirical beliefs. Rational laws? Indeed, like it or not, we have centuries of experience to inform us about the merits of a lawful, non-spiritual, scientific viewpoint.

On the other hand, disbelief in a supreme being comes at a substantial human cost. Disbelievers suffer the lack of certain knowledge about life-ever-after for starters. Sir Arthur Eddington in *The Nature of the Physical World* put it this way: "There are some to whom the sense of a divine presence irradiating the soul is one of the most obvious things of experience. In their view a man without this sense is to be regarded as we regard a man without a sense of humor. The absence is a kind of mental deficiency."[16]

Putting aside personal deficiencies for the moment, I readily admit to being a religious alien because I reject theological thinking in all its forms and functions. From the time of my budding awareness to the present, much of the world—as represented by history and fairy tales, fiction and nonfiction books, society and the media, politics, movies, lectures, you name it—has made it clear how wrong I am in this regard, but I don't just persist in passively disbelieving in theology. I actively reject the notion that religion has much of anything to recommend it. On an imaginary spectrum with theology at one end, metaphysics in the middle, and science at the opposite end, my wavelength is fixed at the ultra-far end of hardcore empiricism.

Sure, I'll admit to being vulnerable to fantastic religious fables as a child, but that all fell apart at about the age of ten. Nevertheless, I will concede a possible saving grace associated with religious conviction. Toward the end of her life, I observed at first hand the emotional comfort faith in a higher power brought to my grandmother. Good for her. Seriously, I would not deprive anyone of a soothing—albeit, in my opinion, absurd—delusion that brings a measure of solace to the poor, disenfranchised, weary, or otherwise needy in spirit, body, or mind.

Back to the idea of laws, there's one that explains why so many people around the world have believed devoutly throughout history in religion while others, like myself, do not believe at all. Such a law was expressed first and most clearly by Francis Bacon way back in his *Novum Organum*, Part XLVI.[17] "The human understanding when it has once adopted an opinion draws all things else to support and agree with it. And though there be a greater number and weight of instances to be found on the other side, yet these it either neglects and despises, or else by some distinction sets aside and rejects; in order that by this great and pernicious predetermination the authority of its former conclusions may remain inviolate."

Pernicious predetermination. Now there's a sonorous phrase that rings as true today as it did in the year 1620, and one that has much to tell us. Bacon's idea can be expressed succinctly using the modern expression, "confirmation bias." The concept applies not only to religion but also to how individuals form and reinforce their political opinions. In essence, once we adopt a viewpoint or belief, we interpret most or all of what we encounter as confirming that belief, and we ignore or dismiss the rest. Both religious believers and nonbelievers tend to be invested in confirmation bias, which can be thought of as an impotent stand-in for critical thinking, especially with respect to someone else's viewpoint.

Sex

I identify as a sexual alien on statistical grounds. I've never experienced a single heterosexual day. To be candid, I did "try it" with the help of recreational Quaaludes (aka Sopers back in the day when the fun pills were handed out casually by dentists and others) with a willing female friend back in college, but the experience did not awaken some dormant or repressed interest in women.

I always thought aspects of human behavior, including sexual behavior, would ultimately be explained through insights gained from chemical and neurophysiological research. For sexual preferences in particular, I expected clarity would come at the genetic level, but I've revised that viewpoint. As to the cause of gayness in particular, let's imagine for the sake of argument that research proved conclusively the disposition is entirely regulated by one or several genes. Would it matter to those who despise homosexuality? Not in the least, I imagine, when fear and condemnation are matters of belief rather than logic or evidence. Would it make life easier for gay people? Doubtful. Thinking, that is, the inclination to use reason, is a choice, as is its absence. "The mind is owned by the self and can make a hell of heaven or a heaven of hell," John Milton suggested centuries ago, but in asking why a person is straight or gay or neither or bi, we are back to the semi-discredited domain of causation.

If causation is a kind of dead end when it comes to quantum physics and sexuality, are there any laws related to sexual preference? Growing up in the city, and then moving to a farm at age nine, I formed my own working hypotheses. I was exposed to two very different cultural worlds at a young age, and the law seemed to be that never in either setting was I as an individual fairly represented, insofar as sexuality was concerned. That is, the person I was becoming, a gay man, was virtually nowhere to be found in books, movies, role models, family or church discussions, in the schoolroom, on the tube, or in any other setting. In fact, the only references I had for that part of the private and internal me were in negative words: fairy, queer, queen, pansy, pervert, degenerate, cocksucker, criminal, homo, fag, faggot, abomination, or the like. If a book or movie back in the day even hinted at the existence of such perversion, the guilty party could be banked on to die by suicide or worse. Moreover, experts who presumably knew the answers, such as members of the American Psychological Association and American Psychiatric Association, identified gay people in those decades as abnormal, diseased, or emotionally disordered, and laws in many states and nations made same-sex relationships criminal. They still do in some cases.

The price tag for a sexual identity ridiculed, persecuted, and apparently alien to everyone and everything around me everywhere I went was, not surprisingly, emotional crisis. Adding to my confusion was the fact that all my life, beginning in elementary school, I've been most at peace in the company of females when it comes to understanding and affection. How could I reconcile such an apparent contradiction? Today, were it in my control I would hand over the reins of political power to women in a flash because, as combative as females can be verbally (another stereotype), I have confidence in a law with all of history on its side, namely that women are generally less warlike than men. There is something in males—from crowing roosters to bugling elk, from head-butting bighorn sheep to hormonal male lions—that wants to fight, even and often to the death. During my life, from grade school to the present, I've found that women make for superior personal, social, travel, and philosophical companionship. Women. I love them, but I do not love them.

But rather than somehow ranking the sexes or sexual preferences in some way, better to think in terms of a little-appreciated law that psychologists, starting with Donald Hebb,[3] proposed decades ago. It states that most behavior reflects both heredity (biology) and the environment. It's not one or the other. We are who we are because of what's inside us and around us. Anyway, one's sex life is personal, and who cares about another person's object of physical desire so long as it's not hurtful?

The Military

Every time I encounter the suggestion on social and other media that we citizens of The Land of the Free should bless and praise all those who have served in the military, I shudder. Let me explain.

It's not that I'm ungrateful or don't wish to honor the memory of the dead or wounded in combat or the selfless in patriotic spirit. One of the principal lessons of history, which can be considered a law according to historians Will and Ariel Durant in *The Lessons of History* centers on the universal human struggle for existence and survival of the fittest in a highly competitive economic world often dominated by war as much as the nobler aspects of human culture.[18] If warfare initiated to gain some (usually financial) advantage is not inevitable, then it has certainly been a predominant, predictable, and consistent aspect of human societies for three thousand years or more. Perhaps it's not surprising then, to see modern nations investing so much time, energy, and money in their militaries and preparations for battle. But when is big enough and good enough really big enough and still good?

Some would suggest the U.S. crossed the boundary from rationality into a twilight zone of combat irrationality soon after World War II. Since that era, war and U.S. warriors have been glorified under the pretense of defending democracy and freedom, or the U.S. Constitution and Bill of Rights, or religious freedom or some other belief system, when actual, political motives are demonstrably centered on money and profit.

Since the year of my birth, the U.S. has engaged almost nonstop either in full-on, active warfare (Korea 1950–53, Laos Civil War 1953–75, Lebanon 1958, Bay of Pigs, Cuba 1961, Vietnam 1965–75, Cambodia 1967–75, Libya 1986, Persian Gulf 1987–88, Gulf War 1990–91, Iraq 1991–2003, Somalia 1992–95, Bosnia 1992–95, Afghanistan 2001–2021, Iraq 2003–11, Pakistan 2004–2019, Somalia 2007–2019, Libya 2011, Iraq 2014–17, Syria 2014–2019, Yemen 2015–2019, Libya 2015–2019) or in covert military operations or one coup or another (Tehran 1953, Thailand 1965–83, Korean DMZ 1966–69, Dominican Civil War 1965–66, Bolivia 1966–67, South Zaire 1978, Gulf of Sidra 1981 and 1986, Lebanese Civil war 1982–84, Grenada 1983, Tobruk 1989, Panama 1989–90, Haiti 1994–95, Kosovo 1998–99, Indian Ocean 2009–2016, Uganda 2011–17). From this list, it seems reasonable to suggest such perpetual military activity goes a step beyond making the world safe for democracy.

It could be argued on financial grounds alone, given the way the U.S. allocates about $600 billion in annual resources, the primary business of the nation is warfare. The French philosopher Henri Bergson maintains in *The Evolution of Life*, "It is then right to say that what we do depends on what we are; but it is necessary to add also that we are, to a certain extent, what we do …."[19] It was Aristotle, however, who first stated we are what we repeatedly do.

What do we do as a nation? Take as an example the number of countries at which the U.S. currently targets its bombs. The count as of this writing is seven. Or take the number of countries to whom we sell armaments while politicians praise the exchanges as good tidings. Take the percent of the Federal budget spent on warring up and warring down the globe. One might argue dollars and cents all day, but how much is enough? Is it enough when most of the national budget supports the military? I am part of the Vietnam War generation that, to this day some 50 years hence, continues to see in the reactions of friends and aging acquaintances how the horrors of that single military fiasco continue to ruin lives.

I am a military alien because I reject virtually everything having to do with the U.S. military as it operates at present. Shall I celebrate young men and women with an overabundance of naïve nationalism and testosterone in their bloodstreams along with a collective death wish of late involving sand and shrapnel? Should I applaud a nation that gives many of its young men the option of either prison or a life-long subsistence wage, on the one hand, or a choice between life-long educational debt versus practical hands-on experience in the killing fields? This is what we're come to, and I deplore it.

Conclusions

When I read a story or novel, plot contributes most to my enjoyment; for nonfiction on the other hand, I hope to learn something or experience something new. No matter the form of the written word however, and partly because I am a writer, the skillful or creative use of language is a key consideration. Others can have completely different and perfectly valid reasons for reading, including an escape from the humdrum world or simply to be entertained.

The experience of an opera for me is all about the music, in particular the beauty of an orchestral score and how well the vocal parts are sung. Because operatic librettos range from absurd in my opinion (Wagner's Tannhäuser) to inane (Mozart's unfinished L'Oca del Cairo), I would not critique an opera for its plot, and while realization including set decoration, lighting, costumes, and staging are all essential operatic elements, it is the music that moves me most. I do not expect other people to share my values about stories or books or music or necessarily to respond favorably to opera at all. No one is trying to sell used cars here.

We live in an era that is astonishing in its offerings and possibilities, at least for the comfortably born and educated, an age of mirror neurons and artificial intelligence. Our most accurate clocks, for example, can tell us whether the super-volcanic mass under Yellowstone National Park is accumulating toward the next eruption. Time by itself can do that. Time, we now understand, is affected by mass (time moves more slowly in a strong gravitational field; thanks, Einstein), and we can currently measure time to better than 17 decimal places. That's astonishing accuracy, and the feat means an imminent Yellowstone eruption will cause local time to slow down enough to measure with state-of-the-art instruments. Truly, the possibilities stemming from human knowledge and gadgetry in science are beyond remarkable, at least to those of us well-enough fed and housed to ponder such matters. But the fact is that many in this world haven't enough food to eat or free time to think about volcanos, let alone take an interest in super-accurate clocks.

There is a broad misunderstanding—or more accurately, a resentment, hence rejection—felt by vast segments of the general public toward science in part because of its association with privilege and higher education. Also contributing to its dismissal is the media's distortion of genuine information into propaganda for mass audiences treated as mindless consumers. The journalist Bill Moyers has repeatedly stated the problem. In essence, it's a blurring on the part of the public and media over what individuals think they want to know versus what they actually need to know to function as an informed electorate. Confirmation bias fulfills the want to the exclusion of the need, and there you have another overarching law.

My personal history has been a search for grace, triggered from a starting line of good fortune and parents who valued education. The search wandered into the terrain of faith at a tender age, then strolled through mediating concepts and intervening variables (such as fate or luck or the libido or soul, all of which are constructs rather than concrete things), and then settled into the landscape of hard science and empirical fact. The journey was made possible because I had the luxury of adequate food and clothing and shelter and time to pursue esoteric interests. Both my parents—the children of immigrant parents—worked diligently to ensure their own two children would enjoy physical security and nourishment for body and brain, including music and a library of books rounded out by the internet of the day, a complete set of encyclopedias. Of all the values to which I was exposed in youth, learning was at the top of the list with my father's constant advice to "apply yourself" to whatever endeavor was at hand, whether tending a vegetable garden, playing classical music on the piano, or painting a picture.

Auguste Comte, in *The Positive Philosophy*, held that the phases of the mind of a man correspond to the epochs of the mind of the race.[20] It's worthwhile to ponder that statement. If Comte is correct, and if what he said is another law of a sort, then we have a second case of ontogeny recapitulating phylogeny, only now in a personal and mental sense rather than merely biological. "Now, each of us is aware," Comte insists, "if he looks back upon his own history, that he was a theologian in his childhood, a metaphysician in his youth, and a natural philosopher [meaning science advocate] in his manhood."

That's essentially the story of my life, though it's also true some of us got stuck in our early thinking while grasping for meaning in a complicated world. I too believed those old Jonah and Noah stories as a child—didn't we all take myths and metaphors literally at first?—until I started asking impertinent questions about the chemistry and dimensions of a whale's digestive track. Then I turned for a time to horoscopes and star signs, to fate and spirits and luck, and to the murky landscape of the "mind" until the value of such intervening concepts tarnished. In the end, the scientific method presented itself to me as the clear winner and man's best friend for understanding himself and everything around him.

Something in that last sentence qualifies me as a permanent resident alien in several ways these days, a religious and political alien to many members of my extended family, more than a few friends, approximately one-half of the voting public, and to all those confident in their convictions about topics ranging from original sin to life everlasting. But whether there is a God or not, whether straight or gay, soldier or pacifist, the issue is how to behave in this world of opinions hotly divided over just about everything under the sun.

I don't expect others to convert to atheism or homosexuality, though it would be better if there were less condemnation of opposing viewpoints. I anticipate mankind will not change its warring ways anytime soon because of my personal aversion to bullets. How to behave then? It doesn't take a genius: the answer is to feel empathy and behave with compassion. Confucius championed empathy 2,400 years ago, and the Dali Lama repeatedly advocates compassion today. There ought to be a law.

Part 3. Wordplay

Exercise

A moment

Drying off on Egyptian cotton, someone eyes him, naked, triggering self-conscious circuits on a cirrus afternoon. Thirty-odd years of pondering blameworthiness coalesce, prompting a thought that people will believe just about anything, or is it *absolutely* anything when it comes to other people? While his hands rummage for deodorant in a sports bag, his brain sifts images, testing beliefs about belief as an engine powering judgments about judgment.

Mind's eye I

He could say his mate is ill. He could disclose that the person he loves above all else in the world is dying and add that the terminal diagnosis is prostate cancer to see if amendment encourages understanding, empathy, or something else. In himself, from others.

After crossing the lot to a mid-size crossover parked some distance from other vehicles, he snugs the seat belt. His eyelids close, weighted.

Mind's eye II

Bas-relief carvings return sunlight and shadow to advantage from two arched, wooden doors that swing open at angles. He envisions walking down the center aisle as Bach's Passacaglia in C Minor concludes, turning to face a congregation he knows and does not know, voice uneven as moisture glosses baby blues and a shudder unhinges his six-foot-three frame. Watching him, hearing him, are friends and neighbors, people that good people call good, struggling to rebound from organ spasms and reluctant airways.

He rehearses the quickest route to a pharmacy that sells a case with lock and key ideal for syringes and a vial. Plus pills round and oblong for good measure. He can leave the case on a nightstand, the key to one side and contents exposed, options of last resort for the ill and tormented to embrace at arm's reach. A solution to the solution? The truth is complex, he suspects, while questioning whether it is possible to elucidate a necessary truth about actual lovers judged unnatural, suffering real afflictions or faltering emotionally. An understanding outside himself and within: what would that knowledge be like?

In the unimagined world

After the usual 10-kilometer run on a treadmill equipped with too many bells and whistles, he showers and dries off on an oversize Egyptian cotton towel supplied gratis by the upscale health club—or ostensibly gratis. In the locker room, he spots someone eyeing him, naked. That is how it started.

This is how it ends

He drives home to embrace his real love and wife of eight years, kiss his daughter, and cradle the baby just turned two months. He is hale, revered, and curious enough to invoke a thought experiment regarding a bridge between beliefs about the world and moral judgment about people, or a chasm. Because he knows he does not know but still wants to know, he flashes again on the disenfranchised, minorities, homeless, illegals, wondering if judgment (from within, without) is a manifestation of belief (e.g., judge not) or whether a gulf separates the two (burn in hell). He notices sunshine outside and takes the family for an outing to the neighborhood playground, a walk a word and a world away.

Extrapolation

What if the music is only in our heads?

What if Mom says you must love family because they are your blood, and
>blood is reason enough.

What if your relative has a bunker of ammo for when libtards come to get his guns, and
>it's true that giving everyone, sane or otherwise, a gun will
deter violence.

What if the neighbors don't vaccinate their kids because if vaccines work, then
>you have nothing to worry about, and, besides,
epidemiology, like climate change, is a hoax.

What if God created heaven and earth, and
>He hates homos because
gays want to turn others homo, and
God's true children need to rid the world of fags.

What if black lives don't matter, and
>the rich earned their billions because they worked for every
penny, and
people on welfare are cheaters, and
poor people are lazy as hell, and
women are inferior to men, and
they all need to learn to mind their betters.

What if Internet hopes and prayers work, and
>poetry's a waste of time, and
the world cannot have too many people, and
numbers lie because mathematicians are in league with the
devil, and
the economy can grow forever, and

fate controls everything, and
everything happens for a reason, and
you can't change people's minds

Because teachers made your brain get grumpy, and glutins made your
ass go lumpy.
Plus those blasted rednecks ate all the meatballs.
But what if everything you think is wrong.

Or

What if everything you think is right, and God is just, and
five men own as much as half the world's population,
as five men do now,
or two men own two-thirds, or
one Man owns everything, and
        poor people drop dead from sloth, and
        meat-eaters choke from gluttony, and
        gun haters perish from Second Amendment indignation, and
        gun lovers kick the bucket from hubris, and
        nobody knows anything, and
        immigrants drown from covetousness, and
        bankers gag from greed, and
        libertines hemorrhage from lust, and
        conservatives expire of extremism, and
        snowflakes melt from progressive retardedness, and
        minorities suffocate from uppity arrogance, and
        fags die of sheer queer perversity, and
        everyone else croaks of indifference, and

God is great and karma is real and everything happens for a reason, and
the one Man remaining on Earth looks over all He has made, and
He sees that it is very good.

Nine Other Lives

Nine

A few evening hours at a restaurant, then an opera: that's how we knew each other a decade ago after being introduced by a mutual friend. Despite the limited time in one another's presence, these days we both draw energy from something akin to willingness bolstered by an implicit accord. Every year she prefaces one handwritten communication to me with a declaration along familiar lines. "As you know—for I've told you—yours is the card I most look forward to receiving." Her departure for a job in Oregon abridged our relationship to once-a-year, long-distance holiday greetings, but what greetings! She calls me her Prince, Dearest, and I address her as Turtledove or Lambkin. The frivolous salutations come with an edge, referencing a post-performance conversation one evening over martinis about how thrilled her parents would have been had their only middle-aged daughter, a doctor, ever married. For fun then, over the miles we cast one another in imaginary roles we could never fulfill, and exchange personal news and views—witty or sad, sometimes down and dirty—about careers, despairs, and aspirations. Just an hour or so each year for nine years running now, putting antediluvian pen to paper, and in my head I feel closer to my December pen pal than to some members of an extended family.

Eight

I keep thinking my relatives are much like anybody else's kin, but then something like this happens. As a working adult living within a few miles of several in-law moochers, my nephew has decided welfare recipients are cheaters robbing honest folks of the taxes they are forced to pay. He uses social media to project his opinions about antisocial justice and the NRA on the collective conscience. Once, he loaded one of his many guns and sat in a dark room. Then while pointing the muzzle at the camera lens, he made his eyes bulgy while somebody snapped his picture. It was one of those weeks when folks were asking themselves for the nth time what might be done about another slaughter of children in yet another blood-splattered American school. At the peak of national grief, up went his image on social media to alert friends and others that my nephew is a man with a plan. Step 1. Aim a loaded gun. Step 2. Wait for somebody to embark on a crime. Step 3. Snap a picture and pull the trigger. Problem solved, at least for a criminal stumbling into my nephew's line of fire. For consolation I remind myself again how dark energy and dark matter constitute 95% of the universe.

Seven

For seven decades, employees at a national R&D laboratory in California have been required by the government to apply for and obtain security clearances. During my tape-recorded interview for a clearance, a young interviewer asked me a question while reading from a script: "We are given to understand you are gay. How often do you have sex with underage boys?" I asked the examiner first to explain how sexual preference might be relevant to work as a science writer, and told the interviewer I would answer the question if every employee—straight or gay—were required to respond to an equivalent question about having sex with children, in the interest of national security. The interviewer switched off the recorder and invited me to step outside for a breath of fresh air. I was offered an apology for the pre-scripted questions tailored for me. When the recording session resumed, the question about underage boys was not repeated. I was granted a security clearance and informed the matter of sexual preference would not be raised again. Perhaps decision-makers concluded I was an unlikely candidate for blackmail, but that is speculation.

Six

One department head, several tenured faculty members, and a student representative conducted the initial interview for my second teaching job at a university. Following an invited presentation on campus, a phone call several weeks later instructed me to, "Get that hot little bottom of yours on a plane and out here." Helen, the department head on the telephone, had a reputation for speaking her mind, and she did not suffer fools. She was also a beer-drinking, chain-smoking lesbian with a robust sense of humor—a "big frog in a little puddle," as she once described herself to me. We formed an immediate bond. Knowing about her reputation for generating gravitational waves in our corner of the ivory tower, I observed two distinct responses to her activities on campus. Students respected her as an enthusiastic teacher and pioneering woman who had been one of the first females to earn a doctoral degree in her area of specialization and then ascend to a position of authority in the academic world. Indeed, she was the only female to sit on the Chairmen and Department Heads committee. Many male colleagues, on the other hand, despised her, and I believe more than a few felt deeply threatened by a woman in a position of power. Some males vented their animosity through behaviors so petty as to suggest hatred bordering on insanity. Many of Helen's allies became my own, and her antagonists mine as well. Some of the brightest individuals I've known in life have been the most childish when reacting to women who outshine them.

Five

An undergraduate student appeared at my front door one Saturday morning, saying she had some questions about the assignment I'd given in class that week. She hugged a bundle of notes to her body while standing outside the entry, dressed in clothing appropriate for midwinter Montana weather. Could she come in? I showed her into the living room and told her to relax for a few minutes while excusing myself to finish shaving in the bathroom. When I returned to the living room, the student had indulged in the offer of hospitality by lounging on the couch, stripped down to brazier and panties. As a large individual, particularly sizeable in frontal aspect, her enormous breasts seemed to spill out of her brazier and overflow onto the sofa. I explained I did not have sex with students. Years later, I related the incident to a friend who asked me, "Is that sexual harassment?"

Four

The principal characters have joined the choir invisible, so opportunities for prosecution or recrimination are long gone. In my role as department chairperson, an older student once came to my office to explain a problem behind closed doors. Her voice shook as she described a colleague who had demanded sex in exchange for a good grade. "I am a married woman," she repeated to me, going on to say she had yet to take one remaining course to complete her major, and the required course was taught by the propositioning professor. She refused to enroll in the class even if it meant sacrificing her major after years of study. I immediately authorized a substitute class, though such a move technically exceeded my authority, and scheduled a meeting with the University President. After informing my superior about the misconduct complaint—and the fact that other female students had independently related essentially the same tale—the President held both hands in the air, palms forward, as a signal for me to cease and desist. There were only two legal grounds for terminating a tenured professor, he said: incompetence and moral turpitude. "Unless you have proof guaranteed to hold up in court, I can do nothing. The University might be financially ruined by damages accruing from a successful counter lawsuit of this nature." So what would the institution require as legal proof in the present instance? Well, for example, the President answered, photographic evidence of faculty–student coitus in the classroom would do. Such was the response to complaints of sexual harassment or assault on campus by tenured faculty members against female students at the time. My warm opinion of the academic tenure system cooled that day and has remained chilly ever since. It was the 70s. More specifically, it was what might be called the era of female liberation cum sexual harassment in the 70s when, sometimes, wrong won and right lost despite earnest intentions.

Three

During the peak of the Vietnam War years, I drew number 63 in the mandatory draft lottery held for all male U.S. citizens of combat age. Within a few months, I received a letter to appear at the County Draft Board and was ushered into the office of an elderly woman who told me to take a seat. The woman came directly to the point.

"Our rural county is sparsely populated, so we don't get many monthly calls, but I expect your lottery number 63 will be called soon."

"How soon?"

She shrugged. "Not many in our county graduate from college, and fewer go on to graduate school, as you are doing."

I nodded.

"As I see it, you have three options."

"Three?" I waited.

"You can go to Canada. You can go to jail. You can teach. Teaching qualifies you for deferral."

The woman behind the desk stared at me and did not mention the fourth, obvious option. That afternoon, I secured my first teaching job and was never drafted into the military. I lost 20 pounds from nervous frustration during the next year of trying to teach high school biology and physics classes, but that's not a complaint. What I do regret is never thanking the woman whose suggestions might well have saved me from the battlefield or PTSD outcomes visited upon so many friends and acquaintances during that era.

Two

My twenty-something-year-old friend loved two things above all else in life: laughter and a good cream-filled donut. Not any donut, but the cream-filled ones sold before 9 a.m. at a certain donut shop in town. While still a college student, this woman would sometimes get out of bed in the middle of the night to whip up a bowl of butter and sugar frosting in the kitchen, then scarf it down. That was before encountering the donut of her dreams and becoming a teacher. One morning on her way to teach at an elementary school a few miles from home, she drove out of her way to purchase a dozen cream-filled donuts at her favorite place. She ate a donut in the car, then another. They were so delicious, she had a third donut while walking to the school building and then finished the box of cream-filled donuts before the first morning bell rang. Waves of nausea sent her to the bathroom where she transferred all the donuts from her private to the institution's public plumbing. After telling the school principal she was feeling a bit under the weather and needed to return home for the day, my friend drove to her favorite donut shop and bought a dozen cream-filled donuts, devouring the first on her walk from the car to her house and several more in the kitchen. She laughs about it to this day and fancies she has learned greater self-control.

One

In the Lithuanian countryside of her nineteenth-century youth, my grandmother lived among peasant households that welcomed as blessings opportunities for child labor to supplement starvation incomes.

Accordingly, my Babo moved into and worked at a priest's residence from the age of seven. She learned to read and write in her home-away-from-home, but in later life she told anecdotes about resident priests dining extravagantly and guzzling wine from silver goblets while her family and friends sometimes went hungry. In the small hours, Babo would occasionally steal into the estate larder and sip wine to get tipsy with another house maiden, but more often, she'd load eggs and bread into an apron, then scurry across frozen midnight fields to deliver food staples to her family. In adulthood, she hadn't a good word for the clergy, but on her deathbed, Grandmother prayed to the one and only merciful God she knew. I find myself unable to believe in the things Babo accepted on faith, and value instead critical thinking, but I suspect we can increase in some personal way from almost everyone who crosses our path. That is to say, we can increase ourselves rather than feel reduced when people—clever or foolish, intentionally or otherwise—reinforce or diminish us while doing what it is they do.

Maybe Three People

He is just turned fourteen going on egocentric and poses in the dark. His black tee shirt fluoresces lettering caught by a camera flash. The message:

All I care about is my guitar and like maybe three people.

In the comment section under this updated social networking photo I type, "I'll remember the sentiment next Christmas," meaning not the guitar part but the three-people part. I anticipate my young nephew will not get it, and he does not get it. From this portrait of teenage solipsism, I consider

Some things I care about

The sunrise interval between REM and bushy-tailedness, that semi-hallucinogenic interlude when nonverbal images boogie without restraint. Will I remember? Outside, clean sheets snap on the line to telegraph an approaching outburst. Speaking of which,

Petrichor

Despite an overabundance
    in recent decades
Of meteorological
    metaphors,
I don't want to know about
    the scent of rain.
Neither the scientific name nor
    its chemistry.
Rather to understand loyalty,
    addiction,
why plants planted equally grow
    unequally,
and human consciousness.

I want to know
    what happens

when the brain hiccups making
   thought backfire
before revving up again as if
   nothing happened.
A cure for greed and losing a soulmate
   decades too soon:
Why on Earth not, and why,
   why?
But not the scent of rain because
   that aroma
needs no increase.

What isn't there

By Friday noon, I anticipate the hour of 5 pm when the weekend starts peek-a-booing around a corner with previews of coming attractions. Ahead are moments of tomorrow imagined, including a performance of the Sibelius Second Symphony and a reminder of the comment the composer made while attending a rehearsal (sans one trumpet player out with the flu) of his work before fleeing.

"I can only hear the trumpet that isn't there, and I can't stand it any longer."

What isn't there: the prospect keeps ricocheting in my head of the kid who was trounced in a playground down the street earlier this week, hoping he will pick himself up from the dirt and discover his passion despite feeling today only what is missing. Or the next great novel or a disappearing high rise with concealed supports, exterior glass, sky-blue ceilings, and earth-tone floors. Look and it isn't there, or is it?

My brother

Because he is the only one left who remembers that time it snowed two feet and we built forts in the yard. His presence reminds every cell in my body of childhood. Sometimes I don't have to explain anything to him, yet he believes that no one has an issue any more with gay people, bless his heart, or if they do, it's *their* problem. Gazing out an airplane window at the horizon, hiking in the mountains, or visiting almost any other uninhabited place, when tilting my head for an altered perspective rendering the ordinary extraordinary, I wonder what it might feel like if people didn't have so much trouble with "those people," other people.

Reminding me of annoyances

Honestly, the truth is that I understand what my nephew means. Simple. Sports fans and fannies out there in cutoffs with navel rolls and backsides leaking over elastic waistbands caught on camera chanting USA! USA! USA!

Ooo-rah! Hoo-ah! Boo-yah! YEE-hah!

What phooey. No wonder some people abroad frown at some people abroad. Throw in cinema-goers rattling paper bags to extract a kernel of popcorn, one at a time, then into the maw with lips agape for tongue-smacking reverberations: auditory runners-up to the hacking hairball squad. Or adult expressions of "Mommy, Mommy! Watch me!" (cute at age six, less so at twenty-six or thirty-six) epitomized by that grunter who carts a gallon jug of water around the gym because a quart is insufficiently pretentious.

Enough snarling. On the dawn of my sixth year my Mom asked what type of birthday cake I would like. Lemon, I tell her, decorated to look like a merry-go-round, please. Mom shepherds me back into the kitchen a couple hours later for my first major disconnect between expectation and reality. No 3D carousel with horses prancing under a canopy; instead, I see splotches of blue and pink frosting for "ponies" (Mom, running short of food coloring, was no artist) plus some lines radiating from the middle, apparently to simulate motion.

Yes, I get your complaints, Sibelius and nephew, regarding what you care about or don't, what is there and what is missing, but one mustn't look a gift horse in the mouth either, and, definitely, we should reconsider the whole business of expectations. Reset, kid, I advise the younger me at age six, and bring it down a notch.

I will get into bed tonight wondering again about testicle-shrinking preoccupations with guns and The Almighty and Our Great Nation— bless our troops—which seem to be conceptually linked. I will think about topics recently huge inside my nephew's skull. And all the thinking will reinforce a personal conviction that it seems never possible for believers to accumulate sufficient firepower to feel secure at home or at the mall, Our Father watching over us from heaven or not. A personal, wallet-size neutron bomb might do the trick? I will reflect as well on trophy hunters, grizzly hunters, cougar hunters, people hunters. Hunters. Then, as is often the case before sleep, I will review the people I've lost in Ohio, Montana, California, numbering many dozens at present, not including the hundred-plus pals and acquaintances taken over in Viet Nam so long ago and by AIDS during the eighties and nineties, every single one too young, and

I cared about every one of them.

Better to think about something positive or neutral. Animal crackers. I doze off.

Paronomasia, Op. 5

According to Ovid, the son of a river god found himself transformed into a flower, but the boy's name rippled downstream from the headwaters of history. If narcissism smacks of partisan conceit nowadays, little reflection is needed to interpret narcissistic as the slurred sound bite of a boozer babbling during booking.

Lots of words have minds of their own and want only a smidgeon of latitude to flaunt alternative applications. It's hardly duplicity when entities flee convention to explore foreign terrain. As in: What ails him today? Answer: *Indonesia.*

Palliatives? A Jamaican run, Singapore fling, Irish jig, perfect Manhattan, plaster of Paris.

With minimal encouragement, numbers play loose with imagination as well. If four equals half of eight no matter what, why does fourteen manifest only half the maturity of eighteen human years? Stranger things happen when digits inflate. Two billion dollars or three: what's the difference?

When words develop egos derived from private lives, undercurrents emerge. Thus, hetero thinks itself a mighty-fine combining form, whereas gay has become flighty by reputation owing to accusations of looking for love in all the wrong places. Buffoon grins through its tears. Zest stood head and shoulders above zit long before those old soap commercials on the boobtube.

Boobtube, of course, is not a valid combo. It's a state of mind implied when words link up to flaunt their stuff at a party.

Stuff? Unlike "stuff"—which is anything it wants to be—there is no term at all for the day after tomorrow or dreams of flying with falcons or operating a vehicle with unresponsive brakes. What about driving but remembering zip between points A and B? Roadlaps? For that stuffed toy hanging from a rear-view mirror (carpet?) or a song in the head that won't quit (tunestick?). For irksome voids in language, why not employ the lexicon at hand? Suggested entries from the *Book of Groans*:

algebra:	shy mermaid's form-fitting top
amusing:	comic's mindset when off athinking
bamboos:	wicked good moonshine

before:	what she be after she be three
benign:	five years after before
bifurcate:	K. Middleton's personal shopper
buccaneer:	cheapest tickets at a shindig
cantankerous:	itinerant people
claptrap:	disagreeable brothel
contour:	one-way bus ride to the pen
detach:	what peasants use on de roof
dispose:	Brittany's barfy pic of Tiffany on Facebook
discuss:	Tiffany's angry oath for being dissed
disrobe:	desirable alternative to dat robe
faucet:	familiar posture at Middle East peace talks
gaggle:	to accidently inhale while gargling
incarceration:	stabbed in a Honda
incinerator:	priest keeping score of a female's confession
locomotive:	grabbing up swampland to make a fortune
malarkey:	sings better than ma ducky
mango:	the act of strangling a husband
mushroom:	stuffy igloo
pomegranate:	every rock climber's horror
punctuation:	gang member's induction ceremony
sink:	snot a pencil
stonehenged:	undone by bitchin' weed
thorny:	lisper's excuse for a cane
truncate:	what the blasted termites did to my maple
tuna:	Boston Symphony's principal oboist
vine:	vaat every vino vonts
yucca:	outburst if you touch one and get a pricka

What happens if you drop a couple of candidates into a sentence? They paid a buccaneer just in time to hear the tuna. Or how about three? After her contour and swearing off sugar, she finally admitted mango to the incinerator. Four? Five? Joyce Carol Oates suggests fiction should make readers squirm, but it is possible to carry things too far.

Cool has lost the fashion edge just as moist vies for top dog in appeal. Pin is fast; pan is slow; pun takes the middle ground. Silk is faster than wool. If pin were drag-racing wool, you could wager a paycheck on the outcome.

Words are packaged with a quantum of smarts. Banal is sophisticated, but deep is relatively shallow even when its referent is not. Prescription meds are consistently wiser than street drugs. Proof? Perfluoroalkylpolyether versus poppers: who wins the spelling bee? Strattera versus smack: who gets the Nobel Prize?

Beyond wit and wisdom, words elicit high interest or low that rubs off.

Sharp words trump ignorant, try it and see.
Drop "plinth" at a party. Grunt "shucks" on the job.
Then wait for the fallout all
casually.

Flavor too.

Argon seems sweet enough, thallium savory.
Serve some on crackers to guests
periodically.

Hot words or tepid, the long and short is that words always have meaning, often more than one. With a possible exception. Some people don't think life has meaning. Your life: no meaning? Use it in a sentence. Put the sentence in a poem, the poem in a book crammed with words having minds of their own. *Voila!* Just from rubbing shoulders, meaning. If that approach doesn't cure your Indonesia, take your carpet for a ride and get some good vine, then swing by and listen to malarkey 'n detach. Hi five, Ms. Oates!

Post Hoc Ergo Propter Hoc

Ta-Nehisi Coates, We Were Eight Years in Power, p. 88

Art [has] no responsibility to be hopeful or optimistic or make anyone feel better about the world. It must reflect the world ... not in hopes of changing it but in the mean and selfish desire to not be enrolled in its lie.

American Association for the Advancement of Science, Feb 3

Satellite and tide-gauge data confirm mean sea levels are not just rising globally, but, according to the AAAS, the amount of yearly increase is accelerating.

Zolfo Springs, Florida, Feb 5

"Infinity Vista" is the name selected by the Board of Directors for 23 acres of treeless swampland in central Florida, divided into 184 one-eighth acre "estates." The property is being marketed by developers to "Bob and Betty Buyer" who won't understand the development's cute name but "will like how the words sound."

Aunt Jan's FacePage. posted Feb 6

Those polar ice caps are getting bigger not smaller at both ends if you want to know what's really happening. That's how all the photos show it from outer space on the news. It's the 4,000 scientists hired by Al Gore and Hillary Clinton to make a killing at the movies who are lying through their teeth because they get paid to scare us to death.

Aunt Jan's FacePage posted Feb 7

A thousand years ago the carbon levels were a zillion times higher, and it wasn't any warmer than today. Look at your fur bears and saber-tooth cats and how big the ferns grew back then with all that carbon in your ice cores from the North Pole. You don't hear all those college people telling you that when they talk about global warming because it isn't true, and they know it. Plants grow better with more carbon, so it's good for world hunger. Kill carbon and you kill off plants.

Environmental Protection Agency, Mar 3

The Head of the EPA today issued a national policy advisory identifying cigarette smoke as beneficial to plant life, "which thrives on carbon dioxide or monoxide, whatever, as everybody knows."

EPA, Mar 4

The EPA today released an amended advisory identifying cigarette smoke as nonhazardous to human health, which is what they meant to announce in the first place.

Aunt Jan's FacePage Mar 5

Smoking never harmed anybody. It's the job you have that pays you money that buys those opioid pills that make you high that kill you, damn those union people to hell. People kill people, that's the way it's always been, and besides, my granddaddy smoked and drank bourbon all his life until Jesus called him to heaven when he was 80 years old, so explain that.

Department of Defense, Mar 14

The DOD has linked increases in skin and pancreatic cancer in the United States to Patagonian dissidents protesting oil exploration in the nation's Puerto Deseado region.

Alabamassippi State House, Mar 17

The Governor announced this morning any skin tone darker than Starbucks® Macchiato is punishable by incarceration for 5 years. "Let's just cut to the chase," the Governor urged, adding the measure would save taxpayers "all the expenses associated with processing individual defendants in custody through habeas corpus" before sending them directly to labor camps.

Aunt Jan's FacePage, Mar 19

Vaccines don't protect you from any a those damn disease things either. It's your hopes and prayers on the Internet that climb the stairs to heaven to sit right where He sits on a throne with His mighty white hair streaming down His robe who looks like George Clooney, only wiser, and rewards your adoration of Him with a long and blessed life that gives you your long life. Besides, vaccines are proven to cause Asperger's Syndrome from eating raw carrots. Just look at my half-sister's kid if you don't believe it.

District Board of Education, March 22

A survey of Washington DC high school seniors revealed this week that 47 percent believe Patagonia is located somewhere around the District of Columbia beltway.

The Executive Office, Washington D.C., Mar 30, a few year ago

"A free press is the lying enemy of the people and will become a poisonous footnote in American history." Forty percent of the nation's citizens support this statement.

National Rifle Association, Apr 1, this year

The NRA endorses a Constitutional Amendment granting blind children the God-given right to shoot any kind of dumb animal they please.

Texas School Board, Apr 8

In a storm of decisions "raining down on classrooms like holy turds from Jesus," according to a liberal news source, the Texas State Board of Education adopted new standards on Thursday, including a requirement that textbooks name The Almighty as the nation's Founding Father, and Patagonia as a fascist state.

From The Addendum to the Dictionary of Obscure Sorrows by Jody Collins, age 11, Plano, Texas, after another school shooting, Apr 11

Will I be remembered more for what I've done in this world or what was done to me?

The Restored Church of God, April 17

According to Disembodied Mathematicians for Christ, 2 plus 2 do not necessarily equal 4, proving planet Earth is 8214 years old. To align with that fact, members of the Texas School Board voted unanimously to revise all arithmetic books used in public schools.

Aunt Jan's FacePage, Apr 19

Anyways I'm sure you all remember that heat spell last summer we thought would go on forever when I prayed for rain, and guess what? It rained cats and dogs and cooled off by 20 degrees, so explain that with your climate change if you want to try.

Aunt Jan's FacePage, May 11

We should bring back all those jobs in the factories like when coal was free to burn and they allowed coal tar to go into the water because everybody knows it never did harm to anybody.

American Families Research Council (AFRC), June 4

Fagmasks® manufactured by the AFRC went on sale today after that organization published "proof" breathing unfiltered air in the vicinity of a homo makes you queer. Proceeds from mask sales will be donated to Electroconvulsive Shock, Inc., a therapeutic rehabilitation consortium. The organization is developing anti-Patagonia masks for production in September.

Aunt Jan's FacePage, June 16

And don't get me started on those doctors out there who call it their practice, and that's what it is. Practice for sure. Who else would make a customer wait on those metal chairs for hours then charge you a couple hundred dollars for three minutes of saying just go on home now and take an aspirin or something? Plus paying thousands for health insurance at work. A racket is what it is.

Columbus, Ohio, second Monday in October

The Ohio State Legislature today passed funding for a statue of Christopher Columbus on the Statehouse lawn to commemorate his discovery of Daylight Savings Time that gives white American farmers an extra hour for harvesting crops.

Jody Collins, age 11, Lubbock, Texas, Oct 16

Every nation that ever started a war has the same thing in common. Men were in charge.

Aunt Jan's FacePage, Oct 27

So I go to my fast-food to get some fries, and guess what? The lazy-ass jerks who think they deserve as much pay per hour as I make after 20 years on the job can't even get my order right. They're over there flippin' burgers and yapping and listening to some hoochie mama radio station that can't even speak American, and guess what? Another crazy-ass kid at the cash register can't make change is what, but she thinks flippin' burgers and not making change she deserves as much per hour as I do after 30 years working my ass off every single day.

European Union, Nov 13

Following a unanimous vote by member nations, the manufacture and sales of motor vehicles operated by gasoline engines will be banned in the EU after 2025.

The White House, Nov 14

The President today signed an Executive Order designating the European Union as a terrorist organization, "along with Patagonia, obviously."

State Department, Nov 15

A spokesperson for the U.S. Department of State issued a declaration this morning that yesterday never happened. Any claim that yesterday took place, according to the release, "is a hoax." The declaration gained credibility when Patagonia could not be reached for comment.

Aunt Jan's FacePage, Nov 17

OK, so now they're out there saying Thug Lives Matter. Excuse me, but no they don't because those Patagonians who go out there and riot how Thug Lives Matter in the streets are all just thugs plain and simple.

Aunt Jan's FacePage, final entry before storming the U.S. Capitol on January 6

Everything happens for a reason.

Ernst Mayr, biologist, paraphrasing something he wrote

Higher intelligence may be an evolutionary error incapable of surviving for more than a passing moment of evolutionary time.

Dinner 1959

Dinner every day of the year is at 6 p.m. sharp. That doesn't mean 6:05.

Having your dinner requires sitting at the big table in your designated chair. Otherwise no food until tomorrow morning. Period.

Table rules are few but firm. Eat your vegetables. Clean your plate. Sit still. Until. You. Are. Excused.

No one says anything when Mother cooks liver and onions for dinner. No one likes liver and onions, but Mother says a doctor tells in a magazine how liver and onions are good for you, so hush and eat what's on your plate.

Anyone still having questions about dinner rules, go read that *Reader's Digest®* article on benefits—for young'uns (sic) especially—when American Families eat together at the table. Unless you have something against family unity, sticking to a schedule, manners, improved communication, and greater respect for others? Very well then.

No one is worried when Mother first announces Aunt Cee-Cee, who is regarded as the toughest nut in the family tree, will be arriving for dinner. At least no one says out loud he or she is upset because, looking on the bright side, it's a chance for everybody to work on interpersonal communication with an elder, isn't it? Cee-Cee is driving all the way from Chicago by herself and will be spending a few days and nights, so everybody just relax.

One person is uncomfortable after realizing Aunt Cee-Cee and Uncle Walter—who drives his big, new car about 90 miles an hour on back roads and often shows up for dinner just in the nick of time—will likely be sharing a meal at the same table tonight. The two have not spoken to one another for "eons." So, we'll just have to see.

If Cee-Cee is a tough nut, her opinion of brother Walter is hard to fault. She thinks Walter is a loud and obnoxious jerk who is uninformed to the point of ignorance and is also a sexist, arrogant, egotistical, bigoted womanizer. Cee-Cee is sometimes wrong, but not always.

Yes, Aunt Cee-Cee and Uncle Walter both make it to the table in time for dinner. They take their chairs but do not look at one another. That is a bad sign.

At least one person at the dinner table is uncomfortable when Uncle

Walter starts in on "them boogies" again at dinnertime, describing for the umpteenth time how those people is always sucking on cigarettes and slurping sickening-sweet bottles of coca cola through straws for lunch at the lunch counter during lunch break at the factory where Uncle Walter works as a security guard. Uncle Walter does not consider cigarettes and cokes a proper lunch for people, and he wishes there were a law, but then "them boogies aren't normal people," so ....

One person at the table, the youngest family member who adores his fourth-grade teacher, wonders what his teacher, an articulate black woman in her 40s, would say if she were present at the family dinner table tonight and heard Uncle Walter talk about "boogies" in 1959 America.

Two people at the dinner table squirm when Uncle Walter tells his two young nephews at the table how he intends to teach them how to "walk like an Indian" through the woods. Walking silently on the forest floor out back behind the house, he means, so as not to scare animals away you want to hunt. Like an Indian. Because Uncle Walter claims he is descended from silent-walking Indians, though no one in the family other than Uncle Walter wants to hunt or has ever heard anything about, or makes claims to, Native American lineage resulting in a predisposition to slip silently through the woods. Still, Uncle Walter swears loudly he is one-seventh Indian. Not one fourth or one eighth. One seventh.

Three people at the dinner table become fretful when Aunt Cee-Cee directs a question to her brother, Uncle Walter, a question that changes the subject and charges the atmosphere. "Are you still humping that spic squaw?"

This is a triple-loaded question from Cee-Cee involving wordplay. It is calculated to get a reaction because it is pregnant with not-so-subtle references to Walter's life-long promiscuity, problematic claim to Indian blood, and racism directed at persons with ancestry other than his own, but especially at people of color, other than Native Americans, whom Walter has never thought of as people of color.

Many adults at the table are afraid Uncle Walter will answer Aunt Cee-Cee by bringing up one of several whispered-about facts concerning her lifestyle. This is fertile territory. For instance, Cee-Cee sells illegal but highly profitable French postcards (you know, porn, some whisper) from behind the counter of her smoke-shop cubicle on a high-traffic downtown Chicago street corner located in a high-crime neighborhood. Also, her shop is the only one on the street that has never been robbed, a remarkable immunity to crime that is not luck but owing to the watchful eyes of Men in Blue with whom Cee-Cee is on the most familiar personal terms and to whom she regularly makes "cash donations."

No one in the family brings up Sputnik. No one brings up Cee-Cee's "mobster" boyfriend connections, or Walter's crazy driving habits in his brand-new, green Pontiac Bonneville coup, which will not remain pristine for long plus he can't afford it on his piddling salary, but don't ask, or how Dad gets peevish after spending time around Uncle Walter or Aunt Cee-Cee, let alone both, or Mother's inclinations to strictly Biblical (nonmetaphorical) interpretations of Jonah and the Whale and The Last Supper.

All at the table, kids included, are relieved when Mother stands up before Uncle Walter or Aunt Cee-Cee can say another word and announces, "That's enough!" while excusing the young ones from the dinner table even before dessert is served, though the kids will get their dessert later. Dessert is a chocolate-frosted, triple-layer, made-from-scratch marble cake over which Uncle Walter, remaining at the table, will ladle cold gravy while eyeing Cee-Cee and claiming he loves gravy on cake—*always* has—just to get Cee-Cee's goat.

Countering Semantic Poison

Once upon turbid waters, the Cuyahoga River caught fire in Cleveland, Ohio, and moms—mine and many others—believed Lake Erie, into which the river oozed during the 1950s, was a source of polio. These days, some swear atmospheric carbon overload is BS, and global warming is a "chinki" plot. One might react to such notions by railing against ethnic or climatological ignorance, but Shakespeare demonstrated a knack for superior wit and syntax in a heavenly quip from *A Midsummer Night's Dream*: "My soul is in the sky." The bard didn't have climate change in mind, but his choice of words shows how it is possible to elevate thinking, or at least the tone of dialogue.

In everyday life, fiery interactions among friends and family members are frequently fueled by linguistic choices and interpretations of meaning. We think. We believe. Moreover, we think that what we believe with conviction is true, but often in the heat of the moment fail to consider underlying currents channeling how an expression is phrased and received. Rapid-fire rejoinders do not generally arise from a foundation of verifiable evidence.

One person's personal or political truth differs from another's, and we all tend toward bias when emotionally aroused. So what are some alternatives to venting verbal venom as a countermeasure when confronted with conversational caca? Are there helpful ground rules or examples?

A case can be made that at least three words in the English language should not be used at all in civil discourse among kith and kin, let alone strangers: the "N" word, the "C" word, and the "F" word for fag. Of course they *are* used with sundry justifications conjuring cultural, creative, comic, or constitutional rights. But regardless of partisan persuasion, wit, or lack thereof, "... right and wrong are fuzzy concepts," as Isaac Asimov observed. Less ambiguous are the advantages of minding one's words and weighing their implications. A sense of humor bolstered by willingness to tolerate some ambiguity or irony doesn't hurt either, but we adore rationalization when indulging rhetorical biases.

" ... Hamlet ... never once doubts the reality of the ghost," D. F. Wallace remarked. Many souls drifting among us today do not doubt the validity of bogus issues, such as a conspiratorial prohibition by the left against wishing someone a merry Christmas, or the perception of near-universal anti-intellectualism and racism among conservatives. Both camps are guilty of confirmation bias, and plenty of kindred ethers cloaked in conceptual certitude haunt the drafty corridors of many a settled mind.

The issue isn't so much good cop versus bad or right versus wrong but, rather, some forethought regarding decency in expression. In matters of contempt versus civility, examples abound in literature and related arts and sciences that transcend—or at least pre-date—the manufactured problem of political correctness much in the manufactured news of our ostensibly "post-truth" era.

Let's play a game and turn base expressions, or churlish or insupportable ones, around. The following table offers examples of verbal or tacit alternatives to conversational incivility.

Alternatives to Poison

Darker conceit	Brighter idea
Epithets	
Ni**er!	Barbaric yawp (W. Whitman)
Feminazi	If the word [concept] doesn't exist, invent it (Baudelaire)
C*nt	Gentlemen do not like forward girls (M. Mitchell)
All fags are sure to go to hell	Abhorred Styx, the flood of deadly hate (J. Milton)
Wingnut, redneck, libtard, wacko, nutjob, moonbat, snowflake, thug, troll	If you can't answer a man's arguments ... you can still call him a vile name (Elbert Hubbard)
Beliefs	
Mine is the one and only true God	Man...makes gods by the dozen (De Montaigne, *Essays*)
My beliefs and absolute truth are one	God and the imagination are one (Wallace Stevens)

The only true faith is blind faith	Reality can be beaten with enough imagination (Twain)
Intelligent design and creationism	If facts don't fit the theory, change the facts (Einstein)
Welfare is sucking the economy dry	I was hungry and you gave me food (Matthew 25:35)
I support the disenfranchised	Love the poor? Name them. (Fr. Gustavo Gutierrez)
Perfectionism is anal	God is in the details (Mies van der Rohe)
Alternative facts	Empirical (per Merriam-Webster dictionary) evidence
(Pseudo) Science	
The unfalsifiable; "proving" the null hypothesis	Statistical uncertainty and certainty (in all science)
Anybody can write anything nowadays	Peer-reviewed articles (e.g., *Nature, Science, JAMA*)
Anybody can say or argue anything nowadays	The Baloney Detection Kit (Carl Sagan)
Everything is a choice arising from free will	Humans = 100% nature + 100% nurture (D. Hebb)
post hoc ergo propter hoc	Correlation does not imply causation (logic)
We know so much now	Multiverses, dark matter, dark energy (astrophysics)
Comic Relief	
Excessive cleavage or plumber's crack	Everyone likes to look down on someone (B. Weeks)
I'll bet you anything that …	Materialists and madmen never have doubts (G.K. Chesterton)
Haggis	Cheetos®
Social and Cultural Propositions	
Determine never to be idle (Thomas Jefferson)	*In Praise of Idleness & Other Essays* (Bertrand Russell)

There is nothing better than hard work	Life must be lived as play (Plato, F. Schiller)
Wisdom of the common man	The best argument against democracy is a five-minute conversation with the average voter (Churchill)
Argumentum ad hominem	Critical thinking is thinking about your thinking while you're thinking (R. W. Paul)
Bookstores are obsolete	Fiction is a necessity (on literature, C.K. Chesterton)
Hate-talk radio and Internet bunk	We shall meet in the place where there is no darkness (G. Orwell)
"No, you're the hypocrite," said the hypocrite	The psychology of projection (Freud and company)
Cyber thoughts and prayers	The Internet can make you stupid (N. Carr)
Ad saturation and rampant commercialism	Ask yourself: is this useful? (*Minimalism*: A documentary film)
Nonstop warfare against (anything)	An eye for an eye makes the whole world blind (Gandhi)
USA, USA, USA!	Nationalism has a way of oppressing others (Chomsky)
Hell of urban living (if rural)	Perks of urban living (if urban)
Hell of living rural (if urban)	Perks of living rural (if rural)
You can never have too much money	For the love of money is the root of all kinds of evil (1 Timothy 6:1 KJV)
Some people don't deserve any money	The lack of money is the root of all evil (Mark Twain)
Money	Everything popular is wrong (Oscar Wilde)
Sure, I do that, but it's not really me	We are what we repeatedly do (Aristotle)

Sources to the table entries—droll to sober—range from Aristotle's musings to Margaret Mitchell's cultural commentary in *Gone With the Wind*. Like coupling Shakespeare's soul-in-the-sky with our contemporary concept of climate change, some items in a given column were not offered originally to address concepts in the adjacent column; nevertheless, pairings may suggest novel, even superior, interpretations of ancient or contemporary epigrams. Are all examples on the left toxic and everything on the right curative? Hardly, depending on context. Are some suggestions gallingly cerebral and others too telegraphic adequately to address nuance? Certainly, but semantics on any level, earthly or celestial, can be entertaining.

At least one individual I know believes guardian angels sporting fluffy, feathered wings flit and flirt among us, and that finding a feather proves an angel is nearby. Nietzsche wrote, "There are various truths, and as a result there is no truth." Well, yes and no, but even the most peevish provocation can be turned on its head with a few well-chosen words.

Part 4. Pretty Fictions: When Words Matter

Truth, as in Fire and Smoke

The landscape

Truth is self-evident, transparent, visible in the footprints on a gumbo track leading to the crime, sworn to and lab-certified, the gold standard, conveyed in the bang of a gavel and clang of a locking jail cell until new DNA evidence comes to light. An amendment is required? Very well. "The truth is rarely pure and never simple."–Oscar Wilde. It is hidden, bendy, elusive, poorly lit and plaintive as the wail of a hungry child in a Mumbai gutter or the forced grin of a gay kid pinning a corsage on the dress of his date to the prom. It is right there in the metaphor about a little pig that builds its house of straw, transcendent as Mahler's Resurrection Symphony, and as final as Dachau. It is paradoxical, blue, and only slightly less troublesome than someone's claim to know the Truth when words are insufficient to describe it. It is your crooked teeth, relative and local, occasionally antisocial, sometimes costing nothing and sometimes dear. Truth has many flavors but is often tainted by personal belief or judgment and easily influenced by emotion: a really great burger for example, or prospects of breaking away early to frolic on a Friday afternoon.

Examples of what people call truth

The world is gloomy and damp, or airy and bright, depending on a person's newt or osprey inclination. "Rutabagas are excellent" is true unless you reject rutabagas. Ditto for the four tenets of evolution, Madonna's genius hits, imagination as a guiding light, the role of human ejecta in climate change, and the Almighty. A poet once wrote, "God and the imagination are one," but if none of many possible interpretations matches your personal truth, buck up, and don't blame rutabagas for your inner newt.

How to know you are telling the truth

A happy truth opens minds, but truth as an unwelcome stranger pisses people off, puts folks on tilt, breeds enemies and crucifixion. If your truth comes uninvited, people might "unfriend" you on Facebook in a modern-day re-enactment of Plutarch's (later, Freud's) "Kill the messenger." Don't be surprised if the person with whom you are having a discussion (1) repeats some point of view, which is that person's truth but not the point, for the third time; or (2) shakes her/his/their head in silence; or (3) bursts into flames. The truth can set you free ... to watch a relationship go up in smoke.

The opposite of truth

Monsters fire-breathing humiliation over the carcass of compassion are runners-up, but anti-arithmetic is the exact opposite. Another exact example is when you huddle alone in a guano-smeared cave dripping with snottites (snotty stalactites) while the walls crumble from another neutron detonation and you chant, "Tomorrow, tomorrow will be better ... ," just as a gun-toting teenager comes at you out of the darkness yelling, "Ni**er!"

Fake and illusory truths

Vanity; comfort from silence when confronted with an outrage because raising a ruckus will do no good; the pretence of taking full responsibility when no action is intended; the illusion of knowledge in the absence of knowing, or certainty that an assertion is always true: these are fake truths. Telling a friend that her full-body pantsuit made of rosemary clippings looks great—"No, really great!"—and those Technicolor insights shooting through the cerebral cortex after a third Percocet or fourth glass of wine: these are illusory truths.

Six reasons people avoid the truth and make up stories instead

1. Your mom never encouraged skydiving, and now it's too late to discover how it feels because you've had to work like a dog for a living all your life.
2. You were refused admission to the college of your first choice ostensibly because of middling test scores, but you know it was actually a case of reverse discrimination, so how are you expected to understand epistemology?

3. You shy away from home improvement because an unmarried cousin toppled off a step stool that came with a 5-star safety rating and fractured her arm in two places when she tried to retrofit a ceiling canister with an energy-efficient LED light bulb.

4. Too many people are poking through trash bins for aluminum cans and plastic bottles nowadays, making a killing at the recycling center, so why are you the one paying outrageous taxes, and what's all this nonsense about the minimum wage?

5. That nephew who re-tweets tweets for kicks about retarded dykes and ridding the planet of trannies is just being a teenager who harbors no ill-will toward anyone, according to his doting relatives, never mind that time he pulled a knife.

6. Your contentious Aunt brought you a salami, the whole salami and nothing but the salami, for your sixth birthday, salami being her favorite food group; at least you seem to recall she gave you salami.

When to stop telling the truth

When everyone has gone up in flames, and no one is left to listen.

Believe You Me

What's the most outlandish statement you've heard a person offer as an opinion the individual nevertheless believes is true? Someone in my clan, after dismissing the value of books, followed up by insisting, "History never happened," and defended the belief. Fantastic assertions that appear to be expressed in earnest invite the question: what's really going on here? Can science provide any insight?

Science, unlike expressions of personal opinion or belief, generates consensus assertions only after accumulating and analyzing evidence. Empirical data (observed through experiments or direct observation) and conclusions from such data are deemed credible in science to the extent the information under peer review meets objective standards for reliability and validity. Reliability is a measure of how consistent and repeatable findings are. Validity is the extent to which procedures measure what they claim to measure and the results can be generalized.

Beliefs are more slippery concepts arising between the fragments of thought and experience. Contemporary philosophers describe a belief as a "propositional attitude" or mental stance. It's frequently a state of mind or attitude involving trust, faith, or confidence about what's not there, or the unknown. Science is about understanding what's really there, as in reality. Science rests on facts or evidence then, whereas people thinking as they please can say or believe any serious or silly thing they want to believe, and they can deny or discount factual evidence that contradicts what they think. The problem with resistance to changing a person's mind in the face of counterevidence is that such stubbornness threatens interpersonal relationships and even society as a whole, especially where human cooperation is crucial.

The distinction between scientific fact and personal belief is reasonably clear-cut then. Scientists value data, and credulous people cherish some of their notions too, especially when it comes to beliefs central to personal identity, but the gullible have no monopoly on balderdash. What are we to make of the following statements attributed to genuine experts, including scientists, over the years?

The French naturalist Jean-André de Luc, who first proposed the term "geology" and advanced the modern concept of geochronology, thought granite boulders came to rest on unlikely spots, such as plateaus in the mountains, after being shot out of caverns by compressed air. Picture a big underground blowgun, and you have the idea. Linus Pauling, the only person to be twice awarded an unshared Nobel Prize, was convinced until his death from cancer that vitamin C cures cancer. These are remarkable claims, but other scientists have made even weirder statements about what they believe.

One of the men responsible for unraveling the double-helical structure of DNA and honored with a Nobel Prize for the work, Francis Crick, maintained without evidence our planet was "deliberately seeded with life by intelligent aliens." William Hershel, the highly regarded astronomer who discovered Uranus and several of Saturn's moons believed aliens living on the sun have giant heads so their noggins don't explode. Another of the greatest scientific minds of the twentieth century, British astronomer Fred Hoyle who was knighted in 1972, suggested human nostrils evolved with the openings facing the ground so that pathogens floating down from outer space wouldn't fall into them. Downright funny, right? Or maybe not?

Perhaps it's less amusing when a politician tells the public a free press is the enemy of the people. It may be depressing or even shocking to hear a leader suggest good people don't go into government or that you can never be too greedy. The problem is that once we adopt a belief as our own, we carry a representation of the belief in our heads—a sort of "belief box" or mental dialogue as some psychologists think of it—and the belief can be taken out of the box and implemented to play an important role in shaping behavior. Accompanying a belief is the potential for real behavior arising from it, but if a belief is false, then action and reaction can become problematic.

What we conclude about a person's beliefs begins to make more sense by pondering the other person's viewpoint—the one holding the belief—but intentions are not always obvious. When an otherwise reputable scientist claims boulders are shot out of the Earth like cannonballs, or the moms and pops of mankind are from outer space, the claimant might just be seeking attention or notoriety. When an expert claims noses point downward to protect against cosmic creepy-crawlers, the objective might be nothing other than to provoke with sheer speculation. When a politician makes ridiculous statements in public, knowing the press will have a field day, the purpose could be simply to instigate, distract, or garner publicity.

Other interpretations, however, come to mind. It's possible a person is genuinely convinced what he or she believes must be true. Is it really so far-fetched to imagine boulders being hurled from the bowels of the Earth? After all, fragmented rocks the size of compact cars have been documented to fly into the air from explosive volcanoes. Is it possible for aliens to have seeded the Earth with the fabric of life delivered in meteors or spaceships? Certainly it is possible. An hypothesis about life being transferred between planets or star systems dates back to the ancient Greeks and is dubbed panspermia. It's also possible the Earth's moon's core is made of cottage cheese or macaroni, though such "hypotheses" aren't scientific propositions because they are not experimentally testable or measurable, at least at the moment. A subject-matter expert might actually believe in an idea that appears on the surface to be ludicrous, but when an authority figure states an unsupported belief, one conclusion is indisputable. A scientist mouthing unsupported personal opinion is no longer speaking as a scientist or from reliable and valid scientific evidence. A politician spewing outrageous ideas is no longer speaking on behalf of the nation as a whole or necessarily in the best interest of humanity.

Beliefs are generally underwritten by feelings. Virtually any emotion—from lust or love to fear and rage—can shape a given belief. For example, we might subconsciously opt to believe in an eternal afterlife to cope with emotional pain associated with loss of a loved one, or to reduce our dread over the certain knowledge one day we too shall die. Throw into the mix one's age, education, political bent, gullibility, ego, aspirations and passions, religious conviction or its absence, anxieties and preoccupations, and it becomes apparent that gut feelings can reinforce or erode opinions we hold dear.

When my distant relative asserted, "History never happened," the conversation had already been politically charged. Context, emotional or otherwise, is not just relevant but usually key to understanding what appear to be nonsensical statements of belief. Here, the unexpected statement was in response to a suggestion the individual might profit from reading a book on a contentious topic. "I don't need to read books," he replied. "Anyone can say or write anything in a book these days. Besides, anything written in books about things happening, say, a hundred years ago is phony. No one knows about any of that stuff. History never happened."

Now to be sure, I like exaggeration in myself far more than in others, as most do, but these are among the most jarringly anti-intellectual remarks I've heard in recent memory. Will and Ariel Durant (*The Story of Civilization*) would surely take exception to the idea of worthlessness of history books in documenting cultural knowledge, but there's little doubt my relative has confidence in what he says. Belief, in short, can be and often is about thin air floating on a foundation of thinner air. In contrast to belief, the only thing that legitimately drives science is empirical evidence, but of course scientists are human too. To the extent a scientist's emotions or ulterior motives affect science, the process is rendered corrupt and unscientific in direct proportion.

A person who renounces book-reading along with the very existence of history appears on the surface to be illogical, even delusional. One might as well claim the universe doesn't exist, but the individual hawking gobbledygook in this case was radically politicized rather than solipsistic. It's one thing if a book-hater deploys the belief by advocating book burning; however, perspective changes entirely when considering some likely underlying motivations. If an individual feels insecure about a lack of book reading or education in general, or feels threatened by opposing viewpoints—in other words, experiences emotions arising from uncertainty or conflict—one of the most common and effective responses is to resort to a defense mechanism, such as denial. In the present context, the internal voice of denial might announce itself along the following lines in response to a perceived threat:

"No, I'm not wrong, you are. If some book says I'm wrong, then books are worthless and so is history."

The argument that anybody can write anything in a book also entails rationalization, which is another common defense mechanism for responding to a perceived threat. Rationalization often involves justifying some attitude or behavior (making excuses) to avoid or hide the real explanation or motive. On factual grounds, a free hand in writing anything one pleases might apply to love letters and blogs and some fiction, but not to historical writing of scholastic merit, or to annotated and peer-reviewed science writing with its emphasis on reliability and validity. It's fair to ask whether the claim made about books being worthless, along with history, is actually about something else.

If a person says for example, "Rats eat garbage and live in it, and they do just fine," to justify neglect of the homeless, the argument is not about rats or garbage. Similarly, statements about books and history being rubbish are about neither books nor history, but instead represent a scorched-earth rebuttal to win at any cost. Discounting the value of all books in this case, and rejecting any new information available in them without even considering the content, is an example of rationalization to maintain a sense of social and political identity.

The same argument can be made about skeptics of science in general or those who appear to reject any science-derived and -validated conclusions. From the examples of celebrated scientists such as Pauling, Crick, and Hershel, it's obvious not all scientists are faultless in their reasoning, and science itself as a discipline is hardly immune to criticism. Indeed, science thrives on criticism. But an individual who disparages the scientific method in general or dismisses all conclusions as worthless to defend a conviction is not making a valid argument against science. Is a rejection of science more likely to arise from intimate familiarity with the scientific method or its opposite? If the latter, then the criticism has little to do with science. Rather, what is being verbalized is a misconception about what someone imagines science to be, or it's about intellectual insecurity along with ignorance of science.

Beyond psychological concepts such as insecurity or denial and rationalization, brain researchers are discovering neural sites and pathways in the brain active in maintaining belief when challenged. Jonas Kaplan, Sarah Gimbel, and Sam Harris have shown alteration in the activity of prefrontal and orbitofrontal cortex as well as emotional and "feeling" (e.g., threat) centers, such as the insula and amygdala, when deeply held political beliefs of test subjects were challenged.[21] Such research verifies an emotional, neurological component underlying certain beliefs.

The Irish writer, teacher, and language activist, Máirtín Ó Cadhain, said (in translation) the year before he died, "We know more about the stars in the firmament than about what's going on under that small skull beside you." Although we are only at the frontier of figuring out the brain's role in maintaining or modifying beliefs, neurophysiological research shows considerable promise in unraveling what's going on at the physical level of neurons. In the meantime, what a person says, especially regarding an inflexible belief, can sometimes reveal more about aspects of character unavailable directly to eye and ear than any literal interpretation of the spoken words.

So what led up to the declaration about books being worthless and history never happening? The trigger had been the idea of splitting, yet another ego defense mechanism. Psychological splitting is sometimes described as polarized or black-and-white thinking in which aspects of the world are split into right and wrong or good and bad, with no allowance for nuances. A person who believes all Republicans are righteous and all Democrats are demons, or vice versa, might hold such a belief to simplify unsettling complexities or to reinforce a sense of self-worth. In response to a suggestion that reading something about splitting might be useful, my relative dismissed both books and history: all books and all of history older than the age of those who today have experienced actual events. The irony—if it can be called irony—is that the mention of one defense mechanism, splitting, was perceived as an attack rather than a path to understanding, initiating the expression of two more defenses, denial and rationalization.

The next time someone makes an outlandish statement in earnest, and before launching a hot or cold rebuttal, we all might do well to remind ourselves about interpreting such remarks literally. What's really going on may not be so much about the words spoken, but rather about what prompts the words. Even when a response appears to be nonsensical, insight can be gained by appreciating the human emotional triggers and neurological foundations underpinning and reinforcing belief.

Enhanced Recollection

First try

I was crawling, and there was a gate. That's about all I can remember.

Second try

Now you ask, I was looking up. Something about being touched, although it's blurry in my mind. What's the point of bringing up the past anyway?

Third

I remember feeling something smooth and cold on my legs, but I don't think recollections like that have symbolic meaning; do you? Why should they mean anything?

Fourth

I didn't tell you I was abused. Even if I was crawling around on the floor, that doesn't mean abuse. Anyway, I don't want to talk about it right now. What's the point of dredging up memories after all this time? Pickles, pickles, pickles, pickles, pickles.

Fifth

Well, someone might have touched me, but I don't know why you keep asking that question. For want of a better explanation, call it repression on my part if you need to give it a name. Or call it dissociative amnesia if you want technical language.

It's like a single line on a painting. First you only see the line. Then maybe a few more lines come into view. It's not clear if the strokes are even in color when you first see them, or whether they might fit together in some way. Then maybe more lines appear, and you start to see the outline of an image. Farther along in time, it looks as if it was always there in the picture—an image I mean—and you ask yourself: why didn't you see it in the first place? You might also ask whether the image is even real or if you're inserting a false memory and you're just making things up.

Sixth

How old was I? That's a tough one to answer because it was so long ago. I can't say exactly, but I think it was before going to school. Maybe it was around kindergarten or even before that because I used to play on the kitchen floor upstairs with my grandmother when both my parents were at work during the daytime. My father had made me a set of wood blocks, and that seems to feel like the right time frame. You see, my mother worked in a factory during the daytime back then, and my grandparents lived on the second floor above ours, so I spent part of the day up there with my grandmother, crawling around and playing with toys on the kitchen floor. It was cold and smooth to the touch, the linoleum. I remember that.

Seventh

I wanted some attention. It was all about attention.

Eighth

On warm mornings, grandmothers in our neighborhood used to wear those long, black dresses. I can still see them. All the old people took advantage of the light out on their front porches to crochet doilies for furniture or to clunk around on floorboards in those big, black shoes while they tended flowerpots. Everybody on our street had big front porches and heavy shoes back then. The really old ones and the infirm sat in rocking chairs, and many afternoons, grandfathers trimmed hedges or tinkered with ancient automobiles or weeded their gardens. These people were Depression Era elders who "made do" with what they had. They saved their nickels, and they all believed that buying new socks when old ones could still be darned amounted to sacrilege. But regardless of seasonal activity outside or the lack, every senior up and down the street I lived on kept an eye out for neighborhood children if they were playing outdoors or walking to school. The elders in our neighborhood spoke with accents, I recall, Polish or Lithuanian, Russian or Armenian, and most knew us kids by name. They believed in discipline. It was a different time.

Ninth

OK, I'll try again. It's mid-morning at a time in my life before I had developed the words to express any feelings. I'm sitting on the kitchen floor made of linoleum, and I catch a glimpse of my grandmother standing as she sometimes did in the kitchen talking to someone else. Maybe she was talking to my father, but I'm not sure exactly who the person was.

I crawl around the floor while playing with toys and realize that I want something. A human touch. I crawl over to my grandmother and reach out for her ankles, feeling the cold linoleum on my knees. Then, as soon as I touch her ankles, I sense a shift in posture, and she goes rigid.

"You nasty boy!" she yells while giving me a cuff. "Such a nasty thing to do!"

But the cuff itself wasn't the hurt. It was something inside that hurt.

Tenth

I didn't know what to say. All I had were the feelings of a child. All I knew was what I wanted. A touch. Yet all my grandmother saw was an imp at her feet, a little devil looking up into her petticoats to get a glimpse of forbidden territory.

"Never, never do that again you nasty boy!"

So here came the cuff across the face. And here came the hurt. Because I had never meant to look up as though I were a thief in the night. Instead of a loving touch, everything got confused. Understanding twisted around, which was the worst part along with not having a way to set things right. It wasn't abuse; it was something else.

"Nasty boy! You have no business looking up there."

That's what she said. And I wanted to say back to her, no, that's wrong. I wanted to tell her what she did that morning had nothing to do with me, but I didn't have the words.

Eleventh

I don't know. I suppose it's possible the entire recollection and my feelings about it now could be manufactured, or what people these days call a false memory. You know, where somebody "remembers" a traumatic experience that never happened. Or maybe it didn't happen the way the individual seems to remember it.

You have to understand my grandmother had ten grandchildren, and I spent more time around her than any of the others from the time I was a toddler. That was partly circumstance because of my age and where everybody lived. The two of us were always close, and doubtless she loved me. But after that day on the floor, something changed. Even at such a young age, something in me died. Or maybe some kind of emotional block was born because I never completely trusted my grandmother again.

Twelfth

Is there a monster here or a victim? I think the answer is no, neither idea applies. What I realize now is that after that morning so long ago, I could never love my grandmother completely. If there was a casualty, maybe it was she because I feared her more and loved her a little less.

Mirror, Mirror on the Soul

Selfless versus selfish. Giving rather than taking. Mahatma Gandhi as opposed to Joseph Stalin. Understanding versus cruelty. Empathy instead of antipathy. Most would agree the first alternative in each of the pairings is preferable to the second.

Although people differ markedly in their capacity to experience or express one feeling or another, a fairly common conviction is that empathy is a desirable human quality. How can we begin objectively to assess a concept as vague as the value of a feeling?

When organisms vary widely along some emotional or behavioral scale, such as a capacity for empathy, it is tempting to propose there must be some underlying mechanism to account for the variation. Darwin applied the rationale to explain variations in physical characteristics such as the body and beak size of finches, and Mendel did something similar for garden peas. As far back as the 14th century, the ex-communicated monk and analytic philosopher William of Occam suggested in his *Suma Logica*e that when presented with competing ideas to explain an observation, according to the principle of parsimony, the simplest explanation is the best.

Is there anything simple about human inclinations toward generosity or meanness? Might there be something universal about feeling as if you know what another person is feeling, or do some individuals lack the ability? Empathy is a complicated social phenomenon having to do with shared feelings, it has been given many definitions, and it has only been investigated in depth by neuroscience relatively recently. Explaining empathy is a tough problem because this so-called trait or disposition can include interpreting or imagining someone else's feelings (a vague word in itself), adopting the perspective of others, or actually experiencing on an emotional level something another person experiences either with or without direct observation.

In a 1990s founding study, Italian researchers doing single-cell recordings and led by Giacomo Rizzolatti and Vittorio Gallese noticed specific cells (10 to 20%) in the premotor area of the frontal lobe of brains—and subsequently in the inferior parietal lobe and superior temporal sulcus—turned on or "fired" when macaque monkeys both performed the action of grasping toward objects and watched other individuals perform the same movement.[22] This type of brain cell, at least in primates at the time, seemed to connect the execution of an action with its observation. Because of the mirroring effect of observation and execution of a motor action in the same neuron groups (seeing and doing), the cells responsible were dubbed "mirror neurons" in early studies. The suggestion at the time was that mirror neurons are engaged both in the actual execution of an action and in understanding a perception about an intention of others to act. Some neurons were also shown to fire when monkeys broke a peanut open or observed someone else breaking a peanut, as well as hearing the sound of a peanut breaking. These types of brain cells were dubbed audio–visual mirror neurons by Rizzolatti and others.

The human ability to feel pain directly as well as to experience the pain of others is one of many suggested characteristics of empathy. Using functional magnetic resonance imaging (fMRI), Tania Singer and her colleagues in a seminal 2004 study showed that both feeling pain and empathizing with the pain of others activated or "recruited" overlapping neurons in the cingulate (toward the midline) and insular cortex (deep within the lateral sulcus) of human volunteers.[23] This study helped to jumpstart the field of social neuroscience.

Since Singer's publication, similar types of neurons have been proposed as playing a role in other affective experiences, such as touching, caressing, and disgust[24] as well as in auditory and visual responses, hinting at multimodal properties of mirror neurons. The mirroring mechanisms for empathic pain and disgust in particular are viewed as similar. Experiments have been done comparing the execution of an action with its observation, imitation, and mere imagination to try to map the neurons in human and nonhuman brains, extending over time to research on animals such as birds and dolphins.[25] The significance of what has become known as the human mirror neuron system (often abbreviated MNS) or network has been downplayed by some neuroscientists and touted by others as one of the most important discoveries to date in neuroscience.

The potential social, psychological, and political implications of mirror neurons are controversial and potentially huge—including a suggestion that they are the basis of human civilization. Such grandiose propositions and other MNS possibilities have led to an exponential increase in scientific papers on the topic, now numbering in the thousands.

Do sweeping hypotheses invoking human civilization have any scientific basis, or are they merely another example of a pretty fiction?

In theory, mirror neuron brain pathways could account for the ability of humans to learn by imitation, recognize other people as human, interpret facial or other emotional expressions, and perhaps underlie social affiliations or antagonisms. The absence of functional mirror neurons has even been hypothesized to account for the dysfunction of social engagement or empathy—dubbed the Broken Mirror hypothesis—speculated to play a role in hot-button issues like autism as well as schizophrenia and psychopathology. Mirror neurons appear to account for the understanding, at least in some people, of what others are experiencing when they see someone laugh or cry for example or withdraw a hand from a flame. "I feel what you feel," appears to have some physical basis, and a related suggestion is that we might understand others more by experiencing or feeling what they feel than by thinking our own thoughts. A central characteristic of empathy according to this idea is the recruiting of mental (cognitive) representations through neuronal and brain pathways that also occur when emotions are directly experienced within an individual.

When it comes to the precise, scientifically verifiable function of mirror neurons or pathways in the human brain, caution is warranted. For example, are mirror cell activities a way we experience or understand another's feelings or simply a sign or reflection that we do in fact understand? In other words, is the so-called "mirror" mechanism how we understand another (a cause) or a manifestation (an effect) of our understanding? We have no unequivocal answers yet to such questions, and there are other problems to unravel as well.

Although many people think of empathy as a single process, psychologists generally agree it is much more complicated, and various types of empathy have been documented. The types include the motor (movement) empathy of the Rizzolatti and Gallese monkeys, the affective (feeling or emotional) empathy of Singer's pain volunteers, and many kinds of cognitive (thinking or perspective-taking) empathy. A more useful idea might be to envision motor, sensory, and cognitive processes as underlying mechanisms with associated neural paths in the brain for empathy rather than as separate types of empathy.[26] In addition, mirror neurons (a motor phenomenon by definition in the early studies) are probably not a requirement for human empathy, which can be generated mentally by just sitting still and thinking or imagining, reading a book or watching a movie, or through learning, socialization, and other means. Moreover, empathy and moral decisions or behaviors are not necessarily linked to one another in any direct way. Moral decisions can be made without empathy, and empathy for others does not ensure good or moral decision-making, or the absence of potential harm or antisocial behavior.

The idea that one person can infer another person's mental state, such as beliefs and desires, through the mirror neuron system has been labeled theory of mind (or ToM, a term criticized as weak and ambiguous by many researchers). The ToM idea appears to be a far cry from the original definition of mirror neurons as representing a motor phenomenon. However, the thinking is that behaviors such as facial expressions recruit mirror mechanisms in an observer, and are then understood in terms of one's own actions, making it possible to predict the mental state of another.[27]

Four types of empathy generally agreed on by current researchers are (1) emphatic concern, the dispositional type of most interest in the present discussion, (2) perspective-taking, involving anticipating the behavior or reactions of others, (3) personal distress, and (4) fantasy. Empathic concern is thought of as a trait or disposition to experience other-person-oriented emotions as, or toward, another person. Considerable psychological research demonstrates that empathic concern has the potential to reduce prejudice, stigmatization, and acrimony while increasing support for such choices as civil rights policies.[28, 29] Thus, empathy is a *trait-like disposition*, whereas compassion or sympathy are emotional *reactions* that might motivate someone to take action.

Given the hyper-partisan nature of governmental gridlock and the acrimony accompanying political elections in the 21st-century U.S., a reasonable question is: to what extent do variations in empathy, including pro-social identity, in our elected political representatives and the public at large account for intergroup conflict between conservatives and liberals? Is it possible some fundamental neurological differences in mirror neurons of the brain for example exist between people who identify politically with either the conservative right or liberal left? Does empathy make us better or more moral? Can an absence of empathy contribute to or even cause political polarization, or can its presence actually fuel divisiveness and trigger antagonism or anger, especially against members of an outgroup? Answers to such questions inhabit complicated terrain bridging psychology, political science, and neuroscience.

As a starting point, research from the University of South Carolina (USC)[30] offers a hint about how people choose a political candidate in the first place. Choices may depend more on our biological makeup than on any critical analysis of the issues, the scientists suggest, because the brains of Republicans and Democrats appear to be wired differently according to their study. Addressing the emerging fields of social and political neuroscience, the USC study focused on mirror neurons in students who had declared their political party affiliations. Resting MRIs in the inferior frontal, supramarginal, and angular gyrus were then recorded to analyze the strength of connections within the mirror neuron system. For declared Democrats, more neuronal activity was found in areas linked with broad (world-at-large) social connectedness, and more activity was linked with tight (family and country) connectedness in Republicans. One possible interpretation is that the two populations process social connectedness in different ways. More generally, how people see the world seems to be a deeply ingrained tendency that might be difficult to modify. However, once again caution is warranted in drawing conclusions because of MRI shortcomings. The MRI data on presumptive mirror neuron pathways related to "social connectedness" are correlational rather than causational, the recorded signals are only an indirect measure of neuronal activity under the scalp, and the resolution covers thousands of brain neurons at once.

Human EEG studies on mirror neurons usually center on mu rhythms (sensorimotor activity) recorded on the scalp. Mu activity decreases during both the execution and observation of movements. Lindsay Oberman and colleagues measured the EEGs of people watching a social-interaction video and found high mirror neuron responses to ingroups (people like themselves) and less responsiveness to outgroups, which has implications for understanding both empathy and prejudice.[6]

If we as individuals have a propensity for empathy for any group, does that make us somehow better, less antisocial, less selfish or greedy, or more moral than others? The problem is that empathy, often viewed as a positive trait, is subject to parochialism and ingroup bias, including ethnicity bias. In general, individuals tend to favor those who they perceive are more connected or more like themselves, and they tend to have more negative perceptions of those belonging to an outgroup who are less like themselves or with whom they are in competition.

Yossi Hasson and colleagues recruited more than 1,000 volunteers from the U.S., Israel, and Germany and asked them to first read an article about people injured at a protest.[31] The article was altered to describe protesters as liberal, conservative, or local residents, and participants in the three conditions answered (1) how much empathy they *wanted* to feel, (2) how much they *actually* felt while reading, and (3) how much they would be willing to help victims by, for example, donating services or money. Results showed that liberals were more likely to want to feel empathy before reading the article, reported feeling more empathy afterward, and reported greater willingness to help (except for Israelis who were equally willing to help either liberal or conservative victims). All volunteers were far more empathetic toward their political ingroup than an outgroup. Such findings along with other studies suggest liberals tend to feel more empathy than do conservatives, but the differences are about more than politics, including a desire to feel certain emotions and how much emotions are actually valued.

Because we often associate empathy with reduced conflict, it may feel counterintuitive to think empathy might actually be a problem, or at least might not always play as positive a role as is often assumed. However, empathic bias in the form of ingroup favoritism can actually widen rather than reduce partisan polarization and distance between social or political groups.

Recent studies by Elizabeth Simas and coworkers measured dispositional empathy in a large, nationally representative sample of more than 1,000 people after taking the Interpersonal Reactivity Index (IRI), which is a well-validated measure of dispositional empathy.[32] The studies show people—especially strongly partisan individuals—who express the greatest concern for others are, in fact, the most socially polarized and likely to increase their dislike or show hostility toward an outgroup. Yet those with high empathic concern and hostility also displayed increased inclination to contact members of the outgroup, compared to people with lower empathic concern.

In one of the Simas studies, more than 1,200 undergraduate student volunteers were shown a short article about a controversial guest speaker representing an opposing political party. Those who scored high on empathy were more inclined to deny the speaker a platform and to be amused by reports of protestors against the speaker injuring a bystander supporting the speaker.

Empathy appears to be contextual and affected by motivation and bias. So for example, ingroup empathy can elevate ill will toward the outgroup, and increased empathic concern can elevate partisan animosity, hatred, and violence. Here, polarization isn't so much about an absence of empathy as it is about the presence of biased empathy. Then again, it should not be particularly surprising that some of the most honored human emotions, including love and empathic concern, are applied selectively given that both can be tiring or expensive in emotional and financial cost.

The verdict is still out on the detailed role of mirror neurons and associated brain pathways in influencing social and political interactions, including empathic concern. What we do know is that there are mirror neuron systems in the human brain, and they likely have some involvement in empathy. With respect to politics, even the pejorative descriptors informally applied by right-wing enthusiasts to left-wing partisans—such as snowflake, tree-hugger, pushover, and libtard—seem to acknowledge subjective feelings of softness or preciousness linked to liberal tendencies to coddle the underdog or to engage in such causes as social justice and environmental conservation. In contrast, conservatives are sometimes perceived as being hard, miserly, or unfeeling and unsympathetic to the suffering of those who look, act, or think differently from the way they do, with an emphasis on authority, law and order, and strong borders. Descriptors such as hawk, oppressor, deplorable, thug (as in re-thug-lican), and fascist are suggestive of an absence of compassion (sympathy for others). In short, many of the subjective and derogatory terms on both sides of the political spectrum point anecdotally to differences in empathy. Future investigations of brain functions associated with mirror neurons could provide more definitive physiological bases accounting for the differences, but it is too early to draw simple conclusions about partisans of one stripe or another having greater or less empathy.

There might well be single neurons in the brain, or groups of neurons working together, or complex neuronal pathways underlying the dispositions we call empathy. As well, there might be a single gene, or several, or complex collections of genes predisposing an individual to, say, asexuality or gayness or straightness as off-the-cuff examples, or predisposing us to love or hate, rejoice or despair. Yet, with or without genetic explanations, some people will continue to disparage gays or support them, some will live their true lives as asexual or promiscuous, and some individuals will feel great empathy or little regardless of what we understand about neuronal predilections to mirror observed actions with feelings or to put mirrored feelings into action.

As biological creatures, everything we are and feel has a biological basis. In that sense, there is nothing surprising about discovering the human brain can mirror the world beyond our own skin, or that strong social or political bonds can elevate empathy or antipathy. Nor is it shocking to verify that antipathy from the outside can sustain or strengthen within-group amity, which can in turn elevate outgroup enmity. What is unsettling is our human inclination to jump to conclusions by imposing "us versus them" labels on people, and the casual obliviousness of many partisans to the nature of their own human nature rather than an informed awareness of that nature. What is promising from a psychological perspective is the insight new research is providing toward our understanding of some of our most complex human traits and emotions.

The Confidence Paradox: Why Popular Views Are So Often Wrong

Ignorance more frequently begets confidence than does knowledge.
— Charles Darwin, Introduction to *The Decent of Man*

In the modern world the stupid are cocksure while the intelligent are full of doubt.
—Bertrand Russell, "The Triumph of Stupidity" in *Mortals and Others*

Angels and auras, glutens and GMOs, assault weapons and Amendment 2, healing crystals and pyramid power, transgenders and gene editing. We might think we know little or a lot about such topics, but what's the objective reality behind all we believe we know about ourselves and the world?

One form of thinking about thinking, called metacognition, is the ability to step back and look with some objectivity at our own behavior and abilities, and perhaps to distinguish accurate judgment from error. Then again, how objective can we really be about ourselves in that way? A potential path is through critical thinking, the intellectual process of analyzing and evaluating, then applying information from observation, experience, or reasoning as a guide to thought and action. An antagonist to objective and critical thinking is belief, which often infuses emotional reactions such as fear, rather than logic, to distort what we suppose is true or untrue.

Growing up in the Midwestern U.S., I remember hearing people claim with emotional conviction the waters of then heavily polluted Lake Erie caused paralysis whereas smoking carried health benefits, and America was deemed a unique land of peace and democracy. At the same time, more than a few politicians and newspaper headlines insisted communists had overrun Washington DC and Hollywood. Homosexuals were arrested as perverts who willfully chose their perversion, recruited and molested little boys, and flagrantly courted the wrath of The Almighty. On many topics supercharged with emotion back then, little ambiguity tempered what folks believed and said. Oh, and by the way, let's all have one more cocktail for the road, shall we?

People following the political news on TV and social media today might be forgiven for supposing self-doubt is in serious decline once again across the home of the brave, or at least at the United States

Capitol, where certainty often bores tunnels through credibility. A national refrain these days seems to honor binary thinking. "I know what you don't know. End of discussion." A problem with this way of thinking is that those who think they know what they do not know, don't know they don't know it.

One way to help understand hollow certainty, especially when it is fueled by emotion along with a decline in objectivity, centers on a type of distorted reasoning called cognitive bias, which can take various forms. It's not a question of whether we as individuals have any mental filters or biases—and if we do, how abnormal we are—but rather how many and how strong are the biases within every one of us as part of the physical and emotional condition of being human.

Here's an eye-opening proposition about one type of cognitive bias. The more we actually know about the real world, the less confident we tend to be in our beliefs and conclusions. Conversely, the less we know in a particular domain, the more confident we tend to be in our beliefs and conclusions. Two psychologists, David Dunning and Justin Kruger, published their seminal research done at Cornell University describing this paradox and highlighting the difficulties incompetent people have in recognizing their own incompetence.[33]

The Dunning–Kruger effect, as it has become known, has been widely cited (thousands of times), sometimes characterized as a possible data artifact, but also replicated in other psychological studies spanning several decades. The effect is a form of cognitive bias in which people of low ability mis-calibrate their own ability and performance. They are convinced of their illusory superiority compared to others who are demonstrably superior, and they mistakenly overestimate their cognitive ability relative to objective criteria. People of relatively high ability however tend to disparage their high ability. How is it possible? One suggestion is that novices or low-ability people do not possess the skills to recognize their incompetence, or to put it in blunt terms, fools are blind to their own foolishness, so incompetent people do not realize how inept they really are. With only a simple idea of how things stand, the tendency is to be over-confident and unaware, and here's the shocker: *ignorance to the ignorant can feel just like expertise.* Furthermore, those with narrow vision seek and adore certainty but often don't receive and incorporate much feedback. Thus, for such individuals the tendency is to believe, "I'm right and you're wrong, so just be quiet."

Perhaps someone in the public sphere comes to mind? Or maybe someone in your private life fits the bill?

A related bias mechanism operates in the opposite direction in above-average folks. The more a competent individual knows, the less confident the person is likely to be, within limits. Of course there are exceptions, such as celebrated experts or geniuses who are egocentric and highly verbal, but in the main, people who pursue a particular topic in depth appreciate how much they still do not know and how much remains to be discovered, so they tend to underestimate their knowledge and ability.

Take the example of someone who decides to pursue a science degree leading to research on vertebrate vision, in other words, how we are able to see the world. The individual might finish a college degree in chemistry, for example, then concentrate in graduate school on psychology, neuroanatomy, and physiology. By focusing on the visual system of the human brain, the area of study narrows even more to specific brain pathways from optic nerves through mid-brain structures called the thalamus and superior colliculi and then to Area 17 of the human cortex. Specialization might proceed to narrower frames of reference, including synaptic electrical impulses and neurotransmitter interactions key to understanding visual nerve signals, perhaps down to the level of molecules. If you asked such a student back in tenth-grade biology to describe how we are able to see, you might get a reasonably confident answer about the eyeball and retina. However, ask the same person as a mid-career researcher, and you might encounter reluctance even to begin to address the question. I can vouch for the last statement because I was the student just described. Indeed, when pursuing any topic toward the limits of human knowledge, it's tempting to conclude we as human beings know relatively little at present compared to what has yet to be explained. Genuine exploration in depth—learning more and more about less and less—often instills modesty rather than certainty along with the idea that a certain amount of confusion can be productive or motivating rather than undesirable.

Intelligence in human beings has been defined in various ways, sometimes controversially, but whatever the definition, the capacity spans a wide range across humanity, often expressed as a score. With a value of 100 dead center (the average or mean value for IQ as it is often expressed), half the population by definition scores less than 100 and half scores higher. Regardless of the merits or faults associated with tagging intelligence with a number, humans clearly vary widely in that capacity. If intelligence is correlated with an ability to recognize one's own cognitive capacity or task performance—in a word, metacognition[34]— then the Dunning–Kruger effect might be extended to suggest those with relatively lower intelligence are likely to be more convinced of their illusory superiority and the accuracy of their mistaken views than those with relatively greater intelligence, who are in general more reluctant to sound off with assurance. If that proposition is correct, and it is only a suggestion, then one can begin to understand how mistaken views often become more widely expressed and disseminated than expert knowledge.

Let's take a few examples of things people think they know—or say they believe—to understand how the confidence paradox plays out in everyday life. The situation often starts with belief bias. Rather than considering the actual merits or complexities of a proposition, belief bias prompts individuals to rationalize almost any information to support a pre-existing belief, and that can be risky. It's one thing to dabble in aromatherapy or to fantasize about imaginary auras for fun, but it's downright foolish or dangerous to infer herbal "detoxification" or magic crystals hold a cure for cancer or dementia because of a belief that true cures must be "natural."

We've all heard one of the most famous phrases in advertising history about milk being good for the body (Got milk?) and more recently, another about glutens being bad for our health. To what extent do we believe the pitches and rally behind them? Sales-targeting by advertisers is so effective that it can lead not only to belief but also to emotional connections with, or reactions against, a given commodity, dietary or otherwise. Think about the implied connection, marketed to young men, between hot sex and racy sports cars for instance. It's more than happenstance that from a young age, most kids exposed to television have heard and seen ubiquitous ads claiming dairy products do a growing body good. In fact, the American Dairy Association, owner of the National Dairy Council, has been touting the health benefits of dairy foods practically since its founding in 1915. Is it any wonder ordinary individuals who are nonexperts in the science of nutrition tend to believe drinking cow's milk is beneficial, and that milk flies off the shelves of supermarkets across the United States? Ask a well-intentioned mom or pop to justify their beliefs about milk, and you're likely to hear something about how milk is just plain good for you; everybody knows that.

But what about human allergies to dairy milk? What about high levels of cholesterol and artery-clogging saturated fat in cow's milk and cheese leading to coronary heart disease, stroke, and, cardiovascular disease? Or consider the estimated 65 to 75 percent of the world's population that is lactose intolerant (a condition far less widespread in Northern European gene pools), let alone the fact that cow's milk evolved as a nutrient for calves rather than for human babies, to say nothing about human adults. The reality is that the benefits of dairy products—promoted by some health organizations as beneficial and disparaged by others as planet- and people-destroying bilge—are controversial and confusing. The bottom line is that health effects associated with consuming dairy products vary widely among individuals, and the jury is still out on a host of potential plusses and minuses.

What about glutens then? Is the consumption of glutens as unhealthy as some people swear? Ask the most ardent detractors what, exactly, a gluten is and many will be unable to explain even basic facts. The word itself conjures an image of a chunky-bottomed overeater, so the stuff must be bad for you, right? In fact, gluten is a mixture of two proteins in grains, such as wheat, barley, and rye, that triggers the autoimmune disorder of celiac disease, which damages the wall of the small intestine. However, according the Mayo Clinic,[35] a source of health information more reliable than many others on or off the internet, scant research has been done on the health benefits (such as weight loss or improved health and athletic performance) of gluten freedom in the majority of people who do not suffer from a gluten-related medical condition. One of many possibilities is that those who identify as gluten-sensitive are reacting to partly absorbed carbs (called FODMAPs for fermentable oligo-, di-, and monosaccharides and polyols) and not gluten at all.

Similar faults in reasoning apply to opinions about genetically modified organisms, or GMOs for short. Individuals adamantly opposed to their production and consumption as food are unlikely to appreciate the widespread reliance of humankind on genetic selection and modification through human history. Genetic modification in plants today involves inserting a specific stretch of DNA into the genome of one plant species, giving it some new and presumably desirable characteristic, such as increased yield or resistance to disease. Genes are introduced into plant cells either as particles coated onto gold or tungsten metal and physically shot into recipient cells or else are introduced by a bacterium. The modified cells are usually grown in culture so they can develop into mature plants and produce seeds inheriting the new DNA. However, humans have been genetically selecting and selectively breeding crops and animals to modify them for various reasons for thousands of years. In the past, it's true cross breeding was limited to similar species, whereas now the constraint no longer applies, and the mechanism differs. In addition, perhaps some antagonists are reminded of the horrors of human eugenics during WWII when contemplating the idea or "slippery slope" of genetic modification in plants today. In any event, heated debate on such topics often invokes political, economic, moral, ethical, and religious arguments, and the paradox is that the most pertinent facts, scientific ones, are often misunderstood or ignored. All too often, disputes arise among people full of intense feeling but little knowledge. That is certainly the case for modern-era anti-vaccination fictions reinforced by belief bias rather than scientific or medical facts.

In confirmation bias, we actively look for ways to justify or defend existing beliefs or preconceptions and ignore or deny conflicting information. Homosexuality is a choice, or it's not. Either way, we're quite sure about it. People who feel most certain that gay people choose to be gay often say they have gay friends, so they cannot be biased. Or they might have a colleague at work who's gay, and they are sure gay people pick their sexuality because "normal" people are heterosexual, besides a friend knows somebody who made the choice to be gay, or a parent is convinced it happens that way, or their pastor says it is so, and the Bible commands a man who sleeps with a man shall be put to death. Such people often ignore what gay people—the real experts—say about the actual experience of growing up gay, namely, their sexual orientation was not an intellectual decision. At least that is the case for me and every LGBT person I've ever known. Indeed, an absence of choice regarding sexual preference makes more sense, given the persecution gays confront from childhood, along with other aversive societal realities.

Either climate change is real, or it's baloney. Let's say a friend or relative claims CO_2 levels on Earth were much higher in the distant past (true, if one goes back 100+ million years), and plants and animals flourished back then, so the whole argument about global warming posing a problem must be a hoax. Genuine climatology however takes into consideration the mind-boggling complexity of climate interactions over time involving ocean temperatures, currents, and chemistry; the sun's energy; earth's reflectivity (albedo) and orbit; volcanic eruptions, atmospheric circulation and concentration of greenhouse gases; organic matter; and myriad other factors. Global climate is different from local weather, yet many continue to confuse the two or do not appreciate the distinction.

It's not unusual in social contexts for someone to raise the idea that cousin Patsy is artistic and Uncle George is logical, so she must be right-brained, and he left-brained. It's true a fundamental principle of brain organization is that the left half of the brain controls the right side of the body, and vice versa. Indeed, every vertebrate brain is pretty much bilaterally symmetrical, with approximately equal left and right halves. It's also the case that about 90 percent of people are right-handed, so what's going on with the two sides of the brain?

In 1871, the French surgeon Paul Broca identified a frontal region of the left hemisphere (the third frontal convolution) vital to generating articulate speech. Soon after in 1874, the German neurologist, Carl Wernicke, described an area of the temporal convolution of the left hemisphere key to comprehending human speech and language. We know Broca's area is connected to Wernicke's area, and damage to the former results in telegraphic speech accompanied by simplistic grammar even though an affected individual can be otherwise clear about an intended message. Ideas about brain laterality therefore have some legitimate anatomical truth behind them.

So, are people basically left-brained or right-brained, as we often hear? According to the belief in brain dominance or laterality, one side of the brain determines personality and behavior so that fact-oriented, analytical people are left-brained, whereas creative and intuitive free-thinkers are right-brained. Furthermore, conventional wisdom according to some people holds getting in touch with our "feeling" (right) brain can promote more positive and creative aspects of being human. Although location in the brain matters greatly for functions such as muscle movement, and people can really be numbers-oriented or art-inclined, scientific research does not bear out the cultural exaggeration of left- versus right-brain dichotomy when it comes to personality.[36] In fact, MRI scans of more than 1000 people's brains and 7000 different brain regions show people mostly use both hemispheres, without dominance and regardless of personality.[37]

What can we say with confidence about personality then? More than 4,000 words in the English language describe human personality traits, impressive testimony to the interest folks have had in the topic. Astrology is an example of what psychologists call a trait or type theory of personality, many of which have been criticized as inadequate to say the least. The pseudoscience of astrology is an example of the Barnum effect (or Forer effect), another bias characterizing the way people tend to see personal specifics in vague statements by filling in the gaps, a propensity for which the human brain is most skillful. Historic examples of other trait theories include the introversion–ambivert–extrovert scale of personality suggested by Carl Jung in the 1920s. It's the old and familiar notion with just a hint of truth proposing introverts are withdrawn while extroverts are outgoing and highly social, and ambiverts are somewhere in the middle. The problem is that such theories (and others from famous psychologists including Carl Rogers, Alfred Adler, Abraham Maslow, Raymond Cattell, and Floyd Henry Allport) are simplistic and inadequate to account for the spectrum of behaviors exhibited by real people in the real world. Often, trait or type theories fail to predict actual behavior in any consistent way from suggested or proposed dominant traits.

Stunning advances in addressing behavioral and health issues have been made on scientific, technological, and medical fronts in recent decades. Accompanying such achievements are absurd claims, fads, magical thinking, and unscrupulous profiteering involving the stars, holistic medicine, placebos, and the like. Open-mindedness to new possibilities and experiences is admirable, but gullibility and ignorance are never praiseworthy. I have a friend who annually scrapes together a pile of money from modest savings to pay for a costly week at a retreat that prohibits phones, radios, and all other forms of vocalization including talking; feeds its clientele a gluten-free diet centered on sprouts and watercress; and designs its daily activity schedules around colonic cleansing and healing-crystal treatments. There is little new here. History rings with accounts of unwise, unpleasant, or downright dangerous "health" treatments involving flesh-eating fish, bat blood, bird feces, leeches, maggots, bee venom, bloodletting, snake-weighting massage, burning towels, human fat (*Axungia hominis*), arsenic hair removal, "miracle" herbal remedies, bogus medical supplements, magic crystals, electrical shock, trephination, and lobotomy to name a few.

My friend gushes about the spa experiences, touting them as

blissfully cleansing and testifying to their powerful health benefits, further reinforcing the well-documented potency of the placebo effect and eagerness with which many humans open wide their pocketbooks willingly to bizarre forms of self-inflicted deprivation and punishment in hopes of some benefit.

A list of phony treatments, holistic cures, and alternative medicines touted through history by unscrupulous merchants and hucksters would fill a small volume, yet people continue to fall victim to rebranded skullduggery in hopes of miracle results. It's understandable if individuals are tempted to suspend disbelief when confronted with a dreadful disease or life-threatening condition, but the cost of misdirection and fakery—in emotional currency, needless suffering, and disappointment—is enormous.

If know-it-alls often know the least and many average folks can be duped, are we destined to remain fools or, at best, undiscerning and gullible? After all, brains are wired generally to take the path of least resistance, which often means doing what we think we know or have done before. The Cornell investigation, described above, explored people's perceptions of their own competence in the test domains of humor comprehension, logical reasoning, and grammar, but they also studied the possibility of helping the most incompetent people—the bottom quartile or lowest-scoring 25%—realize their ineptitude by making test subjects more competent through training designed to improve logical reasoning skills. Such training was successful in several ways. It not only improved test performance scores dramatically over the course of the study but also sharpened the self-assessment of individuals participating in the training. The results point to the importance of feedback—social, critical, quantitative—in revising one's own conclusions by comparing them with reality. Critical thinking, once again, can make a difference.

If the internet and other media abound with spin and fabrication as well as flat-out lies, where can valid and reliable information be found for those willing to take time to look? Perhaps the most important criteria are the credibility and integrity of a source of information. Every area of human interest these days, from astrophysics to abstract art, features subject-matter experts who know the field well even if they do not know everything. The shelves of libraries hold more critically reviewed and award-winning books on wide-ranging topics than any of us will ever take time to peruse. University output, including educational websites and peer-reviewed journals, are among the most trustworthy resources, but on topics ranging from pyramid power to vaccination, it's inevitable to encounter sham sources with legitimate-sounding names offering pre-scripted conclusions masquerading as reliable data. Warning signs are familiar-sounding organizational or professional titles imitating legitimate ones, claims too good to be true, glowing personal testimonials, unsound or unbalanced analysis limited to one side of a complex topic, or issues unduly simplified. The absence of proof does not prove or disprove anything, much like the presence of opinion. Anyone can evaluate a source of information by asking if someone, starting with the author and affiliation, stands to gain by making a particular claim, then remembering how those who claim they know the most often know the least according to the Dunning–Kruger effect. In the end, it might be necessary to swap the seductive allure of absolute certainty in our thinking for the better ambiguity and unease of not being quite so sure about what we think we know.

Conspiracy Theories: Why We Can't Unsee Patterns— Real or Imagined—Once We See Them

Effective conspiracy theories typically capture and hold attention through audacious, often sinister, allegations rooted in emotion rather than an analytical or documented chain of cause and effect. Research on factors associated with conspiracy beliefs, including proposed political and psychological motives, has accelerated in the past decade, and the principal findings are revealing. However, largely ignored in the literature—although addressed in at least one recent cover story on conspiracies[38]—are some underlying considerations that might provide a foundation for human predispositions toward conspiracism, as reflected in the universality of conspiracy theories across cultures and throughout recorded history.

Three additional foundations to conspiratorial belief that I would like to explore here include: (1) the mathematical Ramsey theory, which shows how order (the perception of organization) must invariably appear from apparent disorder; (2) the neurophysiology of signal and pattern recognition underlying the ways vertebrates are "tuned" to detect information that is biologically or evolutionarily adaptive for survival; and (3) a human predisposition to derive and superimpose emotionally meaningful interpretations on sensory input and then to adjust behavior accordingly.

Given the broadly documented emotional quality of conspiracy beliefs, together with additional psychological mechanisms suggested by other investigators—such as biased assimilation and motivated reasoning—conspiracism appears to be a predictable outcome in individuals who may lack or reject more analytical and cognitive tools to arrive at rational explanations for events.

Secret Plots

Conspiracy theories are notions or purported explanations, often with negative connotations, about some event that features a secret, insidious, or fiendish plot as a central feature.[39] The goal of the alleged cabal is often to deceive and manipulate people or to usurp political or economic power. Machiavelli advised in *The Prince* against advancing conspiracy theories because even real conspiracies often fail to achieve desired ends. Modern research points to more troublesome effects, including the sowing of social discord, violence, and public mistrust while undermining constructive discourse on important issues. Even unlikely conspiracy theories can have adverse effects on people's lives, health, and safety.[40]

Actual conspiracies, such as bribery or collusion among team players to throw a championship game, insider trading or schemes to cheat regulatory standards, and plots to rob a bank, involve real events with a documented chain of cause and effect. In contrast, conspiracy theories offer allegations that are often social in origin and outcome, rooted in emotion, diabolical in tone, intuitive rather than analytical, and they may or may not be true.

Despite their adverse consequences, conspiracy beliefs are not limited to fringe groups, and their prevalence cannot be blamed on the internet or social media. Instead, they are pervasive across cultures and throughout recorded history, and they can crop up almost anywhere. Among the more enduring in Western culture are notions about John F. Kennedy's assassination arising from a massive scheme involving the CIA, Russians, Cubans, and the Mafia; NASA moon landings being staged by the government; UFOs and aliens landing on Earth; secret societies controlling nearly everything; and 9/11 as an inside job. A 2016 survey by researchers at Chapman University[41] found the following percentages of Americans who agree or strongly agree that "the government is concealing what they know about…"

The 9/11 attacks	54.3%
The JFK assassination	49.6%
Alien encounters	42.6%
Global warming	42.1%
Plans for a one-world government	32.9%
Obama's birth certificate	30.1%
Death of Antonin Scalia	27.8%
The moon landing	24.2%

It's no exaggeration to suggest almost every major historical event has generated a conspiracy theory. Indeed, enthusiastic conspiracists have occupied high places in society and politics, including the White House.

Although some conspiracy ideas can be credible—or correct in questioning ethics, politics, or society in general, or useful in holding authorities accountable—intentionally mistaken or absurd theories (e.g., QAnon and the satanic pedophile ring that Donald Trump was allegedly combatting) can be harmful to individuals or culture as a whole, often by confusing facts and fiction or fueling hatred. Why are crazy or manipulative conspiracy theories so prevalent? Is it true that certain psychological characteristics cause some people with a so-called "conspiracy mindset" to believe them more than others? Scientific studies addressing these questions have mushroomed in the last decade. Other insights on possible origins of conspiracy theories lie in some relatively underappreciated ideas related to mathematics, biology, and how belief is shaped by human emotion and anxiety.

Do the Math First

Ramsey theory is a branch of mathematics focused on how a degree of order or regularity must appear unavoidably from apparent disorder.[42] Developed by Frank Plumpton Ramsey in the 1920s and expanded considerably by Paul Erdős thereafter,[43] the core idea of Ramsey theory is that random elements fall into specific arrangements. Given enough elements—and it doesn't take many—an interesting pattern is guaranteed to emerge. A surprising example of Ramsey theory centers on people gathering at a party. In any group of at least six people selected at random, the gathering will invariably include three mutual friends or three mutual nonfriends. According to another mathematician, T. S. Motzkin, in writing about Ramsey theory, complete disorder is impossible.[44]

If total disorder can't happen, perhaps it's logical and helpful for us to seek or impose order—or more to the point, purpose or meaning—on the apparent disorder of phenomena we encounter. Could the tendency to perceive underlying design be a biological predisposition (or in evolutionary terms, an adaptive process) with a foundation in mathematics, given the reality that patterns are everywhere, and it might be useful for us to perceive them?

After combined appendix and tonsil surgeries at the age of eight, I remember staring at the acoustic ceiling tiles above my hospital bed during the boring days of recovery. The white tiles had tiny, random holes scattered on the exposed surface, and I found myself picking out images in the distributed holes, much the same way people see features or figures in star clusters on a clear night. Once I identified an image, such as a human face or horse, I couldn't make myself *not* see the pattern on the ceiling. Even at the age of eight, I wondered why, and if it was just me who saw recognizable images where none existed. Was there a name for it? There is.

Connect the Dots

A tendency to detect order in apparent disorder is true not only of humans, but nonhuman animals as well. One term used to describe this phenomenon is *pareidolia*, or the tendency to incorrectly perceive patterns where none exist, such as shapes in clouds, random sounds as words or phrases, or faces in water stains.[45] Another term is *patternicity*, or the tendency to find meaningful patterns in both meaningful and meaningless noise. Patternicity, developed by Michael Shermer, expands on pareidolia inasmuch as many apparently meaningless patterns turn out to be real, just as some conspiracy theories are true, as are many scientific theories first thought by some to represent random anomalies, such as anthropogenic global warming.[46] Two key tools of science, in fact—Signal Detection Theory and its counterpart Statistical Detection Theory—are grounded in the necessity of establishing criteria for detecting signals in noise, such as the well-established p values of 0.05 and 0.01 for determining statistical significance.[47]

The brains of humans and many other animals have been shown to be superbly organized to detect specific signals and patterns. Since the late 1950s, scientists have demonstrated how even a frog's retina is organized to detect distinct features in the world, including sharp edges, curved edges, moving edges, and movements produced by dimming light, akin to shadows.[48] None of this is surprising, given a frog's typical lack of eye and head movement as it sits still on a rock or lily pad, especially when we consider that a frog's survival depends on escaping enemies and snatching bugs from the air. After all, both predators and flying frog food feature dark, moving edges as they pass across a frog's visual field.

Cats are notorious for how they see and respond to the world, including good night vision and a fondness for pouncing on laser pointers or other darting targets. Two neuroscientists, David Hubel and Torsten Wiesel, worked for more than 20 years on visual experiments using cats and then primates as models for human vision.[49, 50] They eventually won the Nobel Prize for their efforts to demonstrate that neurons located at the last stop of the visual pathway, namely cells of the visual cortex in cats and monkeys, are "tuned" to detect highly specific, oriented structures and contours, not unlike edge detection in amphibians.[51] Another important finding was that restricting visual information from reaching the visual brain during a critical period early in the life of a kitten alters electrical activity of the brain's visual cortex. Such losses in processing information are virtually nonexistent in adults who experience visual deprivation for one reason or another later in life, so once present, pattern detection is durable.[52]

All of this is to say that humans and other animals, from amphibians to felines and primates, have evolved over eons to pick out contours and patterns that help individuals survive in a complex world, including edge detection and other types of information. Some of the time, there really is a signal in the noise, and it might be well to sense and perceive it to determine if there is any useful information to be gained and exploited. Maybe the reason we are inclined to detect patterns—at a basic biological level at least—has to do with how the brain itself works. Because our eyes and brains are tuned to perceive features and can hardly avoid seeing them, we might have the beginning of an explanation for why conspiracy theories are so prevalent. We are biologically "tuned" to see features, however functional or fictional. The signal might be useful to us because it represents a predictable pattern, just as it can be useful for survival to recognize the absence of cause and effect.

It isn't just edges or sudden movements humans are engineered to pick out as signals in a seemingly random world that is decidedly not random at all. Human brains are so specialized for detecting facial features that a specific area called the fusiform gyrus (located in the occipitotemporal lobe) is dedicated solely to face recognition, with both sides of the brain equally involved in the task. Different circuits center on familiar versus unfamiliar faces, but other brain areas, including the prefrontal cortex in humans, also respond to faces and interact strongly with emotional parts of the brain, including the amygdala. Single neurons are thought to respond selectively to faces of specific individuals, and the chemical neuropeptide, oxytocin, plays an important role in facilitating face and emotion recognition, of obvious importance in social interactions. More recent studies, however, show that the firing rate of individual face-recognizing cells corresponds to separate facial features along an axis. Different combinations of firing along the axis can create an image of every possible face with remarkable precision.[53] We might think of the brain as a highly complex xylophone or keyboard, with individual keys representing a feature-recognizing brain cell, and faces as complex chords played on the instrument.

Of course, conspiracy theories are about much more than detecting such features as edges, motion, and faces. However, decoding how the brain works to perform fundamental tasks can tell us something important about how we not only recognize stimuli but also process information. Frogs don't simply *see* an edge on an otherwise blank canvas, they attribute *meaning* to the input and behave accordingly. If an edge features sharp contours and moves rapidly, a frog might well conclude it's an insect and tongue-snatch it for lunch. If a moving edge signifies a large predator, such as a swooping bird of prey, a frog might jump to escape. As humans, we don't simply sense a face: we recognize an individual as husband or wife and attribute meaning and intention to facial expressions. A smile signifies we can joke; a frown cautions against responding flippantly.

It's fair to say our brains are designed to pick out signals with meaning or possible intention from apparent noise, and neurons in the temporal lobe perform the tasks unrelentingly even when we are unaware it's happening. When the perception of meaning or connections is mistaken, it's called *apophenia*, of which pareidolia (the incorrect perception of visual objects, such as a horse on ceiling tiles) is a subcategory. Add human emotions, such as fear, and factors like threat and personal beliefs to the way we perceive objects or events in the world, and we have the principal elements of conspiratorial thinking along with the possibility of erroneous attribution. In regulating human responses, the brain is designed to oversee detection and recognition, but emotions imbue perceptions with color and meaning, and emotions are notoriously unreliable when it comes to impartial judgment.

People are more inclined to buy into a conspiracy idea when they feel threat, anxiety, powerlessness, or uncertainty owing to distressing social events. Moreover, according to the social psychologist Dr. Jan-Willem van Prooijen, believing one conspiracy theory doesn't reduce the experience of threat but does the opposite, stimulating additional conspiracy theorizing in a sort of positive-feedback loop.[54] Once a person sees meaningful patterns in dots on the ceiling, the images do not go away. After we see the face of the man in the moon, it's difficult to unsee it.

Once we believe in a given conspiracy theory, it's tempting to see conspiracies operating elsewhere. In fact, the best predictor of belief in one conspiracy theory is belief in another. Given the partisanship, anxiety, and distrust associated with politics in America and elsewhere, plus a disruptive pandemic during 2019–21, some have lamented we are currently experiencing a Golden Age of conspiracy theories.[55] Such claims have been made for decades. Political scientists Joseph Uscinski and Joseph Parent searched through 100 years of over 100,000 letters to the editor featuring conspiracy scares published in *The New York Times*. Their analysis generated three pages worth of conspirators, from Adolf Hitler and the African National Congress to the World Health Organization and Zionist villagers, catalogued into seven types: Left, Right, Communist, Capitalist, Government, Media, and Other. (The last type includes Freemasons, and even scientists and the AMA). Letter writers in the 1890s, for example, were afraid that Mormons had rigged elections for Republicans and that Canada and England were conspiring to reclaim U.S. territory. In the early 1900s, correspondents were worried about the role of financial interests in undermining democracy. And so on throughout the 20th century, dispelling the myth that conspiracism is a recent phenomenon. The common theme running throughout the newspaper letters was *power*. People writing to *The New York Times* editors expressed their concern that someone or something was engaged in getting or using illegitimate power to manipulate others, which is not always a false conspiracy theory.[56]

Who Believes or Doesn't Believe

Although it seems obvious that conspiracy theory beliefs are exacerbated by political partisanship, according to recent investigations there is no simple correlation between left (liberal) or right (conservative) thinking and tendencies to believe or disbelieve in conspiracy theories. Rather, according to Adam Enders and Steven Smallpage, two researchers studying relations between conspiracy theories and politics, we all live on a continuum of conspiratorial thinking with respect to acceptance or rejection.[57] Our beliefs are often formed for good reason, given the way the brain works in looking for connections and the survival benefits of being suspicious or cautious, especially when we feel threatened. Almost all behavior is strategic to some extent, and conspiracy theorizing appears to represent a strategy for responding to threat even if some or all of the underlying details are bunk. Michael Shermer calls this "constructive conspiracism," where enough conspiracy theories are true that it pays to err on the side of assuming most conspiracy theories are real—including false positives—even though many are not.[58]

As a rule, advocates of conspiracy theories are as inclined as anyone else to appear rational and openminded, at least on the surface. In a systematic review of 96 studies on conspiracy beliefs (including 93 studies published since 2007), a variety of human predictors were assessed.[59] Among the personality factors that had been previously suggested by some psychologists as predictors of conspiracy beliefs were low agreeableness and high openness to experience, but neither these nor other personality factors, such as neuroticism, could be verified in the survey as significantly manifest in people who believe in conspiracy theories.

When rational explanations fail in times of uncertainty, however, so do logic and reason in favor of sensationalism, at least for some people. But who is more likely to buy into conspiratorial thinking when experiencing anxiety? Instead of looking at personality traits as predictors, a University of Chicago researcher, Eric Oliver, assessed different styles of thinking. According to Oliver, people fall on a spectrum of thinking from magical or intuitive at one end to rational at the other. An intuitionist tends to think in terms of unobservable or magical forces, relying more on emotions and gut feelings or religious beliefs, and then making judgmental shortcuts while rejecting what's observable to explain an event. A rationalist tends to favor logic, deduction, and facts, while relying on analytical thinking and transparency. Oliver notes that most people (about 60%) are somewhere in the middle, with intuitionists outnumbering rationalists about 2 to 1 in the remaining 40% of people.[60] If the percentage estimates are fairly accurate, then a large segment of the human population, which includes a relatively large number of intuitionists, is susceptible to conspiracy beliefs, and some people might both believe and partly disbelieve. On average, though, a fortune teller or an evangelical is more likely to buy into conspiracy theories than a physicist or statistician.

Beyond underlying personality, psychological motives, and styles of thinking, other researchers have suggested possible demographic factors linked to beliefs in conspiracy theories. They include low education, low income, being male, and being a member of some minority or an "outsider." Confounding variables and other complications place these demographic ideas into the category of suggestions requiring more study.[61]

What's Wrong with Believing, and Why Do People Believe?

What is the problem with being keen on conspiracy theories? According to another comprehensive review of interdisciplinary literature,[62] conspiracy theories do more harm than good. Historically, such ideas are associated with prejudice ("us" versus "them" thinking), genocide, witch hunts, radicalization, extremism, gun ownership, terrorism, and a rejection of mainstream medicine and science, as is manifest in negative attitudes toward safe sex, vaccines, and human-caused climate change.

If conspiracy theories are potentially damaging and sometimes even contradict each other (for example, those who believe the conspiracy theory that Princess Diana was murdered also tend to believe the conspiracy theory that she faked her death) on top of other flaws, why do some people persist in embracing and propagating them? In certain cases, official or authoritative explanations for events are inadequate or contrived to meet political or other objectives, and people know it. There are also professional opinion-makers—including well-known personalities on social media, radio, and television—who make a living by stoking the flames of conspiracism (e.g., Alex Jones), and they can be effective at their jobs. Beyond external factors, do internal psychological mechanisms dispose individuals to believe conspiracy theories? Five mechanisms have been suggested:[62]

1. A desire to discover meaning to counter uncertainty and preserve beliefs. Such information processing is a higher-level (more complex) example of perceiving patterns in seeming randomness, which we know our brains are specialized to do well. Of course, in a hunt for meaning, it's possible to go off the tracks.

2. Biased assimilation—similar to confirmation bias—which refers to a tendency to incorporate information that confirms what we already believe is true, especially when lacking cognitive tools or other skills to arrive at explanations by more rational means.

3. Powerlessness, low status, lack of control, and compensation for failures. Demonizing others can be powerfully reinforcing, especially for those who harbor prejudice or antagonism against certain segments of society. Even if an object of scorn is unspecified, it is convenient to blame others for individual failings as part of a self-healing strategy. After all, if such elusive entities as the Illuminati, the Deep State, powerful corporations, shape-shifting lizards, or plant people control everything, then personal failures—financial or otherwise— are hardly our own fault but, rather, are the predictable outcome of a rigged system.

4. Narcissism and maintenance of a positive self-image. Those who endorse conspiracy theories may feel a need to be perceived as personally unique by possessing rare and important information unknown to other people.

5. Defensiveness and a desire to strengthen group identity by suggesting antagonists are conspiring against the group, especially if the ingroup is undervalued or threatened by an outgroup.

Looking Away

Once seen, we can't easily unsee the man in the moon any more than a frog can ignore a darting insect or we can force our brains to disacknowledge the face of someone we know. Effective conspiracy theories capture attention through audacious claims, sometimes mixing outrageous notions with clever interpretations. They are perverse in flaunting convention, bolstering egos while reinforcing the worst expectations, or explaining what otherwise seems unexplainable by suggesting something shocking and sinister about what we may already suspect is true. When an idea is as entertaining and infuriating, titillating and extreme, reinforcing and loathsome, laughable and egregious, personally elevating and socially destructive as a popular conspiracy theory, chances are good that our interest will be piqued. The irony is that conspiracy theories thrive by assuming proponents know there is the official story, a reported story, and the underlying truth, while what is offered up as conspiratorial truth to well-meaning truth-seekers might well be anything but the truth. Nevertheless, like a highway accident or train wreck, it's difficult to ignore or look away from a good conspiracy theory.

Part 5. Parting Words

When Here and Now Are Gone and Forgotten

Education doesn't necessarily make a person canny, and guidance doesn't automatically deliver insight. A first-rate education can have the opposite result, reinforcing how much a person does not know and likely cannot know. In dealing with degenerative diseases such as dementia, family members otherwise schooled and experienced in the ways of the world may feel they don't know a thing.

Nonprofessional caregivers confronted with the gradual mental failure of a loved one are travelers marooned on a hostile planet without an emotional compass. They are observers dealing with erratic signals received as sights and sounds, behaviors and feelings they cannot parse. Within the alien domain of dementia—where the most mundane experiences can go topsy-turvy without warning—folks come up against an affliction potentially more emotionally destructive over time to the observer than the afflicted. If that idea sounds backwards, consider the hundreds of pamphlets and books written on the subject of coping. Despite well-meaning advice from experts, studious caregivers with earnest intentions—especially husbands and wives, sons or daughters—often feel as if they are smothering or drowning.

A key difficulty associated with responding to dementia has to do with feelings, or what psychologists call "affect." With respect to emotional impacts on those doing their best to help others, the domain is as deeply personal and disturbing as any experience can get. I know something about the place because I've been there. Absent universal guideposts, a few travel notes just might make the journey more endurable for others.

The Four Percent

In college, I read highly regarded literary works and took numerous science classes. Chemistry and astronomy provided a peek at the cosmic origin of atomic elements up to and including iron, which we now appreciate originated from star furnaces. I thought I knew lots of things, but confused big-picture summaries—treated in relatively superficial ways—with deep knowledge.

Several years into grad school, I found myself hunched over a microscopic to peer at a mini-niche of the known universe. My interest in neuropsychology narrowed to tiny areas of the visual and emotional systems, such as the amygdala, and from that micro-perspective, I gained a sense of what advanced study is and is not. Graduate work involves formulating a good question about the unknown that can be answered through research, but it's not a matter of getting to know a lot about a lot. Instead, the effect is to gain some appreciation for the scope of information we humans lack within the narrowest field of vision, deep inside the big picture. Whether a person is formally taught or self-educated, any rigorous line of inquiry reveals the extent of our individual myopia and humanity's collective ignorance about almost everything.

If the suggestion of collective ignorance smacks of exaggeration, consider what cosmologists tell us today. Roughly 70% of the universe, give or take a few percent, consists of dark energy, and another 26% or thereabouts is dark matter. The murk is so pervasive, yet elusive, that experts have no better language than to apply "dark" as its descriptor. What does cosmology have to do with dementia? Everything we know anything about in the first part of the twenty-first century amounts to about 4% of the universe, and that's not counting the possibility of multiverses. If our present knowledge in the physical sciences can be characterized as relative naïveté, then the same descriptor likely applies to the biological sciences in general and to issues relevant to humans in particular. Human behavior is an especially tough nut to crack.

The way people respond is so intriguing that we like to indulge in both fictional and nonfictional accounts of how individuals live, love, and frequently struggle with failure. Fiction can be challenging because the subject matter requires a writer to imagine situations not entirely real. Nonfiction poses even greater problems by (1) promising truthfulness about real events, as is inherent in the very word "nonfiction," (2) sometimes disclosing personal information or confidences about folks we claim to know well, but probably don't, (3) dealing with issues that may be emotional, and (4) doing it all as if some moral authority grants permission.

As a self-defensive insurance policy, creative nonfiction writers may conceal identities, particularly real names and locations. What follows is an account of three Middle Americans told with as much honesty as is decent. Two identities are obfuscated, but because the third individual is my father, and he died a few years ago, a cloaking device is pointless.

Dad

Did I ever really know the man, even when he was healthy? I wonder.

My father was an emotionally inaccessible parent who eventually succumbed to dementia. As a depression-era child of first-generation immigrants taking root in a soot-belching, steel-belt (now Rustbelt) city, he struggled. A scarcity of money during formative years left permanent wounds, and like many others of his generation, he counted pennies, until he lost the ability to count anything. He yearned to finish college but did not return to the classroom after a first son was born, then a second. Though encouraged by a publishing house in New York City, his novel never saw print owing in part to the untimely death of his publisher-champion in a plane crash.

What I surmise about my father's reality derives mostly from behaviors I witnessed firsthand. Perhaps his greatest success in life centered on marrying a good wife: the pair enjoyed a fine relationship for more than six decades. For his part, I observed a soft-spoken and humane individual, a classical-music lover and avid reader who valued education above almost everything else. I believe his early years served as a lifelong wellspring for suspicion and angst. Over time, he grew more antisocial and distrustful of folks other than my mother and me. What I did not appreciate until discovering some personal letters he wrote in his late twenties were the heartfelt feelings he conveyed to Mom: his soul not quite, but almost, laid bare. In those letters, he wrote with genuine passion about the devotion he felt toward his young wife and two sons, along with career misgivings and aspirations.

The man I once thought I knew, and subsequently didn't know at all, died at the age of 92½ after what was mostly a good life. And, yes, I did not know my father at all after he succumbed to a condition diagnosed as vascular dementia, one essentially indistinguishable in behavioral expression from Alzheimer's disease. Tiny blood vessels rupture, and with each insult another part of the brain goes dark, together with whatever behavior that part manages.

I am not inclined to clinical depression, but I came to appreciate what that illness means after my father's condition passed the point of rational return. I know things many others don't know about dementia and parenting a parent—principally what my dad's life was like during those last few years before and after he had to be relocated into residential care from my home, where I had served as sole caregiver. I also know what my life became during that time. For example, I understand that it really matters: what we say and do not say. It matters: what is done and what is not done for an individual whose brain is failing. Yet the amount I do not understand is breathtaking.

Most of us are adept at assumptions. We assume a person is smart about one thing or dumb about another, kind or hateful. It's common to believe that we can grasp a situation and deal with a given problem, to rationalize and imagine things won't be quite so bad after all and that we can afford whatever cost or burden a particular difficulty presents. What's the worst that can happen? We shrug and get on with it especially when options are few. When a life-changing reality comes home, however, especially the crushing reality of irreversible mental decline, a major challenge is to appreciate the moment when all bets are off, and any advantage associated with second-guessing is gone. When is that point of no return, exactly?

Are You Aware …?

Two physicians ask me the question in the ER hallway after a brief examination. Are you aware your father has dementia?

Am I aware? Well …duh. I think something along those lines, but don't say it aloud. Instead I describe what I have been dealing with for years, invoking the image of a man on a stepladder. I talk about a plateau in my father's mental functioning and then a step down, another plateau in ability and a step down. Repeat and keep repeating. I use hand gestures because I'm nervous in the ER.

"A good analogy," one doctor says.

"Do you work at a job away from your house?" the second doctor asks me.

"I do."

Two physicians tell me point blank in the hallway, "You can no longer take care of your father."

I protest. I explain that I've done the job of caregiving for years now, that I did so for Mom who died in her own bed from long-term chronic gastrointestinal disease, and I will do the same for Dad. I will do it in my own house and on my own terms, and he too will die in his own bed.

Two nurses repeat essentially the same arguments the doctors just made in the hallway. I desist from responding because, well, what do they know about my personal life and capabilities? A social worker asks me to sit down at her computer and observe. She scrolls though data. Fact sheets. Resources. She talks about falls and injuries. About fires. I stare.

I can do this, I insist. I did it for Mom, though hers was a physical rather than mental ailment. Five staff members gather around me in the ER and repeat the message. You cannot work full time and take care of your father alone. You cannot.

*

My father owns a handgun and keeps it hidden, I know not where. When Mom's illness became terminal, Dad told me he did not want to live after she died. For several years, I came home from work expecting to find him dead on the floor or in the bathtub. That was when he was able to think and act coherently.

Back home from the ER later that night, my father says the same thing he has been repeating almost every day for a year. "I feel like I'm in a fog." He is aware of losing awareness, a once-intelligent man now in distress over waning comprehension. I think such knowledge must be the worst part for him: knowing his brain is lying to him—as all our brains do from time to time—but now in erratic and irreversible ways with no likelihood for improvement.

I cook dinner for us both and serve it at 6:00 p.m. on the dot. We keep to a schedule every day. A routine. I have read all about routines in the literature. A routine makes each day go more smoothly, the literature claims. But Dad starts failing to arrive at the table for meals, asking why are we eating at this hour? Because it's dinnertime, I answer. Why aren't we having breakfast then, he wants to know. It's a strange time to be eating breakfast, he says next, looking out the sunset window. Where is here, and when is now? Is it daylight? He asks questions of that sort in random order, but I have no answers that satisfy him. A schedule seems meaningless when he cannot differentiate between night and day. We might as well be in Ghana or on Ganymede or speaking Jerkin to one another. He dives into dinner, never losing his appetite. Not even at the very end.

I mentally record his increasing failures to comprehend time and place, his loss of numerical ability and orientation in space. Sometimes I have to tell my father where his own three rooms are located in my house.

Then I might need to point the way. He had been spending increasing time sitting at the desk in his living room, at the opposite end of the house from my kitchen. Sitting there for hours, then entire afternoons, days and months on end for more than a year. It's his private place, and I have never peeked into his desk or at his papers because it has been sacrosanct territory throughout his life, and mine. We both understand the rules. But we're on Ganymede now, so one night I do look. I pull out the middle drawer and open his checkbook to encounter chicken scratchings. Acalcula, they call it. It's a loss of mathematical ability, and it's often one of the early skills to go.

I had given him my Acura to drive a few years before, the one with several hundred thousand miles on it, so what would it matter if it got a few dents? More than a few dents later, I ask him leading questions after work, but he quietly, sheepishly denies having any mishaps. He just drives to the local grocery store now. I call the insurance company and get a horrified response from a woman my age. She knows about dementia and reacts predictably.

"You absolutely *must*, blah, blah." "He must *not* blah, blah." "Not any more."

I tell her I know all about it, but driving represents his last means for expressing independence, of a sort. Do I take that away from him too? It is painful to imagine putting the vehicle on Craigslist, but I do, and the car is sold the next afternoon.

Months pass. Home from work late one afternoon, I almost slip on the floor of the mudroom and laundry area that serves as our common entry from the garage. It is flooded. Opening the lid of the washing machine, I find water filled to overflowing and try to extract with much effort towels, fitted and flat sheet sets, two queen-size blankets, and a massive and waterlogged comforter, all of which have jammed the mechanism and rendered it junk.

In the living room, Dad is sitting in a rather odd posture. His elbows and knees are bleeding into a summer shirt and lightweight pants. That afternoon, he went out to the side of the house to collect plums ripening on the neighbor's overhanging tree. He just wanted some plums. While reaching over the fence, he fell and could not get up. He crawled back inside on hands and knees through the garage, laundry room, and kitchen area in his part of the house.

The Worst Days

Our family physician is an astute man who has known us both for years. He asks Dad about any interest in trying some medication that might—just might—help with mental focus or delaying memory loss. We agree to give it a go.

A couple of nights later, Dad enters my bedroom at 3 a.m. and calls my name in the dark. I sit up in bed to hear him explain, "The people upstairs are ready to go." Mine is a single-story ranch house, and we have no travel plans. I rise and usher my father, who is carrying a paper bag packed with clothes, back into his bedroom, explaining that the hour is early and he should try to get some more rest. Pill bottles are spread all over his bathroom floor.

I learn two valuable lessons: never disagree with a person who has dementia, and watch for adverse drug effects. Never contradict because, after all, does it matter whether the world is overpopulated or polar ice is melting or a trip is planned or imaginary? Does anything other than losing your mind matter to a person who is losing his mind? Maybe one thing does matter though: having another person around who cares.

I come home from work to the stench of burning metal. A blue haze fills the hallway and my father's kitchen. Dad is sitting in his living room but cannot smell anything, a lifelong condition. He just wanted to hard-boil some eggs, and he turned a stove burner on high. Now the metal pan relaxes over the surface in the style of a Dali painting, and I disconnect his kitchen appliances at the fuse box and check all the smoke alarms.

I investigate "retirement" and "skilled" nursing homes that are, in a word, deplorable. The odor in some places is enough to propel me back out the door. I tour private residential care facilities next. I interview people, and they interview me. Costs are outrageous. Money does not matter though. Unless you don't have enough. Who has enough? Pause. Well, it is what it is, and a person has to choose.

But wait a second. Might financial assistance come to the rescue? In my neck of the woods, the cost of 24/7 in-home care is more than 100K per year (and that's several years ago). Medicaid? A person in my state can apply only after spending down nearly all the afflicted individual's assets, then get on a waiting list and wait for … how long? Two years, currently. Possibly longer, I am advised. Later I'm told that the state's resources have been exhausted, and we probably would not qualify anyway.

Well then, what exactly *is* covered for dementia? For psychiatric services where I live? For related medication? For practically anything? Sometimes a little; more often nothing.

I move my father into a residential facility located in a decent suburban house in a middle-class neighborhood only about ten minutes distant from my home. The facility has only five patients and what appears to be a competent staff dedicated to personal attention. They suggest we move Dad's own bedroom furniture into what will become his new room that features a private, en suite bathroom. A great idea, I think. The staff's relatives help with the move. Nice. We arrange items, including photos and framed reproductions, to mirror to the extent possible the layout in what was his own bedroom at my house. When he first sees the new room, he remarks, "It's my room!" looking pleased and tired. He wants to rest, so I leave.

Things seem to go well for the first few months. He says the food is fine, and he makes a female friend, which amazes me given his reclusive nature. But as time passes, he starts to make inappropriate sexual remarks to the female staff, which is the antithesis of his once-demure personality. He grabs at them. He escapes outdoors one evening, though the doors are normally locked, and is found down the street trying to enter a locked car. He begins to threaten people, raising his cane toward them. He is a person on flat ground descending a stepladder, with each rupture of a tiny blood vessel in his brain bringing him closer to some location below sea level.

I visit him most days, and pick him up late one morning for our weekly drive to his favorite family restaurant that features a "Senior Menu" with astonishingly low prices. On the return trip, my father appears to be in good humor, but as we pull up to the residential house, his mood darkens. He refuses to get out of the car and keeps repeating that he wants to go home. Caregivers come out and smile encouragement. We bring out his sweet and elderly female pal and tell him to come inside for some cake. Nothing works. He keeps saying he wants to go home. I am late back to work for a meeting and use my cell phone.

Don't contradict, I remember. Never argue. I am sure my father needs to use the bathroom, but what to do next? Distraction?

I re-enter the car and say that I need to stop off at the bank for a minute, which is not the case. I park and walk around the rear of the bank building to puff on a cigarette, and when I return and open the car door, he is furious.

"You've ruined my life! I have nothing. Nothing."

"What should we do?" I ask. "What do you want me to do?"

"I want to go home. I want to be with your mother."

I explain that Mom died six years ago, but he is crying now.

"You killed her. You killed Mother."

When I remind him of what happened and about her terminal illness, he says, "You could have done something. You killed her."

Eventually I am successful in changing the subject and mood, but this is the last time I take him out of the residential care facility for an excursion.

I have difficulty sleeping from then on and feel a species of mental anguish that will not stop. I slide the screen door open and sometimes walk outside to take in the rolling hills that serve as my spectacular backyard view in the Golden State. I try reminding myself that I am fortunate to have all this. The California sun is blinding most days, but that isn't the reason tears stream down my face. It's not the sunlight but an inner torment for which I have no words. The feeling of knowing nothing. I feel like screaming at the sky, at the dirt. At life. Is this how a "nervous breakdown" feels? I always wondered. I think I know.

Sometimes I feel shaky and experience heart palpitations that might be imaginary or real. The world is red some days, or another color or no color. I feel blind. Rage. Empty and overwhelmed. I hear rushing sounds. Silence. I feel utterly hopeless. Helpless.

Hospice, Scribbles, Silence

Hospice agrees to step in, and I learn a few things. I thought I understood palliative care and end-of-life procedures after caretaking my mother and my soul mate and so many others who died of AIDS during the 80's and 90's. I am an intelligent adult who has administered morphine and been around the block. This time however, it's different.

Dad develops skin cancer on his left temple. It turns out to be an aggressive form of cancer that rapidly doubles in size. I tell the hospice nurse that the wound needs treatment, but she disagrees. No point now, she says, but I insist on a physician's visit. The spot doubles in size, then redoubles. Cancer threatens to invade an eye, and I protest. It's too much. I am informed that the hospice nurse instructs the residential staff to "Put a bonnet over the man's head if it bothers the son so much."

I dis-enroll my father from hospice care and call a physician friend who specializes in cancer treatment. *Thank you, Fred.* He tells me exactly what to do, and my father is conveyed from his bed by stretcher and ambulance, because he can no longer walk or stand upright, to a cancer-treatment facility. One of the staff members there whispers the term "elder abuse" in reference to my parent's condition and the hospice response to it. A series of radiological treatments is immediately scheduled, and my dad is transported by stretcher and ambulance to and from the center over the next several months for each treatment. The care is expert, and the treatments are remarkably effective.

I receive a bill for $2,400 for the first medical-transport ride, which is not covered by Medicare or any other insurance, though the agreed transport price was $200. After phoning the ambulance company, they tell me they have no record of any such agreement, so pay up.

I re-enroll Dad in a different hospice program that comes highly recommended, and this time the nurse assigned to Dad is an enormous black dude who is one of the kindest and most attentive humans I have ever met. I want to hug him. I would bless him if I were qualified.

In my father's room, I discover a scrap of wrinkled paper tucked away in a drawer on which he evidently tried to write something to me several months before. The scribble-writing is difficult to make out, but I spend time deciphering it because I expect it must be important. I find it is a warning.

Beware of the (expletive deleted) *woman* (resident Asian caregiver) *who is stealing from me. She will steal from you too. Watch out!!!!!*

Shaky exclamation points are written in a row, something my dad would never have done when coherent. Then the person who was my father stops trying to write and says fewer and fewer words. A couple of simple phrases remain. Eventually, only one word. "Yes." Do you want such and such? "Yes." Are you in any pain? "Yes." Are you better now? "Yes" Worse? "Yes." He was always a stickler for grammar and enunciation, and even now, the word is a perfectly formed "Yes." It's never a yup or yah or uh-huh. Then no words at all. Nothing. Then, finally, labored breathing.

I receive the call one evening and drive over. The short jaunt to my destination from home feels light-years distant. Two men wearing dark suits arrive to wheel my father's body out the door and place it into a hearse. They drive away.

I hug one of the women who has been feeding and cleaning my dad for months. I am overcome by loss, grief, and release.

Jen

It's been a few years since that evening, and now during Christmas holidays I have the freedom to visit friends and family who live back east, including people I've known since graduate school. Jen, divorced and living alone, has been struggling with words for a while, nouns mostly and sometimes verbs. I notice the problem on the phone when she reaches for a term and ends up hesitating before stammering, "… ah … you know … ah …." Sometimes I know, and sometimes I don't, but we have laughing conversations anyway, joking about "Alzies."

Anomia, which is also called anomic or nominal aphasia, is a deficit of expressive language characterized by loss of word retrieval, often nouns and verbs. I learned about it way back in graduate school, right around the time I first met Jen. The condition can develop into a kind of personality theft. In Jen's case, the problem might be the result of a stroke or something else, but she tells me one of her doctors has used the "A" word.

Before I see Jen for Christmas, she tells me on the phone she'd been shopping at a local grocery store and her wallet was stolen from her purse. She was able to file a police report on the spot because officers were already at the scene dealing with another theft moments before. That night Jen drove home from the grocery without a license, and she has not responded to phone calls from credit card companies trying to make contact. She lost her medical insurance and social security cards as well. After arriving at her house Christmas week, I notice a stack of unopened mail on the dining room table. Upon making telephone inquiries, I learn that about $10,000 was charged to half a dozen of her credit cards on the day of the theft, which was two months ago.

Jen does not feel comfortable speaking on the telephone because of her word-retrieval difficulty. I can understand the feelings. She can't come up with answers to questions quickly enough, and it's embarrassing. She can't seem to organize her day or thoughts very well, and she has dissociated from most friends and family members who pay little mind to her situation. Her bathroom sink has been stopped up for half a year, and the plumbing outfit that inspected the problem handed her a $2,400 estimate to tear the hot and cold water pipes out of the tiled wall and replace them—to replace the incoming hot and cold water pipes, no less, when it is the drain that's clogged. She knows the outfit would be ripping her off but has taken no steps to contact other plumbers. $2,400 seems to be a popular tab for people in distress.

I spend the next few days driving Jen to the police department to pick up a copy of the crime report, then around town, including visits to the DMV and her credit union. I do most of the talking. For two more days, we spend hours on the phone with credit card companies. Jen gives each company verbal permission for me to discuss financial matters, to speak on her behalf. We get the drain unclogged for $90 and fix the cable TV modem and remote for no charge. I help with other chores.

Upon returning to my home after the last visit with Jen, I call her to recommend she develop a Living Trust because her old one is decades out of date. I remind her about de-cluttering her house, the basement and attic especially, both jammed with clothing Jen wore back in college plus her parents' furniture and much more. I urge her to tackle one thing at a time. I mail her a Living Trust form. It's critical now to start planning for the future and all that. To start looking into assisted living. To sign a power of attorney for financial affairs.

She knows. After a year, however, she has taken no action.

I think I understand the problem, and I believe Jen does as well. We both realize there's an urgency here, but how does a person start to address all the different issues at once? It's emotional. It's overwhelming.

She knows. I know. We know next to nothing, or maybe about 4%.

Langer

Another person I visit during Christmas (let's call him Langer) lives at the opposite end of Jen's town. We also became close friends during graduate school, and we have taken many trips together over the years. The man has a reputation for lightning wit, faultless logic, and searing insight. Or, rather, he *had* such a reputation.

Langer is a clinical psychologist with a background in neurophysiology. He operates a private practice out of a small building in an artsy business district and does not employ an office staff. A while back, he began neglecting invoices for his patients. After he fell months behind in billing and receiving, his wife noticed. It is not an exaggeration to say that Langer's personal and professional identities are invested in his practice and that his work represents the meaning of his life. Indeed, his expectation—realistic or otherwise—was that he would never retire but continue at least a part-time practice until he died. "It's who I am," he would say.

Langer always had a penchant for losing things, misplacing car keys and the like, but when he began to neglect financial matters and repeated himself in conversation, his wife began to suspect short-term-memory issues. Immediately after the diagnosis of Alzheimer's disease, he was forced to shutter his practice for obvious reasons. That was several years ago. During my most recent visit to Langer's house, one incident suggests how things stand today.

It is the first evening of my holiday visit, and we are at the kitchen counter. Langer's wife must work in the morning and has gone to bed, so it's just the two of us along with two big dogs downstairs in the big house. Langer makes a second drink for me and pours himself a third and fourth. We all know his reaction to liquor, so this is a bad idea. I open the back door to get some air and step out to find the evening unexpectedly mild for this time of year. A neighbor's dog barks somewhere close by, and water cascades down waterfalls into two koi ponds Langer has built to fill his idle days. After about three or four minutes elapse, I re-enter the combo kitchen and family room.

Langer remains standing where I left him next to the counter, but there is something odd about his demeanor. I say that I don't need another drink and would like to retire for the evening.

"Where are you sleeping?" he asks me.

I point a finger upward to the second floor and say I will use the guest bedroom, as I always do. It is an odd question because sleeping arrangements in the house have never changed over the years. I walk around Langer and proceed through the family room only to discover my friend following on my heels. He is much too close, and I feel awkward about it. He continues to tailgate me up the second-floor stairway, and I sense something amiss, but I can't put my finger on it. At the top of the stairs, I bid him good night, but instead of answering, Langer stares at me and continues to watch as I enter the guest bedroom and close the door.

I hear talk from the master bedroom. The commotion appears to be between Langer and his wife, but the volume is scary. After a few minutes, Langer's wife taps on my door, and I come out into the hallway.

"He doesn't know who you are."

Langer's wife is also a clinician, but this is new territory. She leads her husband from the master bedroom out into the hall and explains for the second or third time who I am. His face is hostile, and he shakes his head. I try to think of something that will re-establish a connection, but it's not easy. I remind my friend of our past, of grad school and friends we had in common back in the day. Nothing works. We return to our separate bedrooms for a bad night's sleep.

Say It Again: Emotion

During the "gay-plague" decades in America, I helped usher many friends out of this world, all of whom were far too young to die. I hugged mothers and held hands and went to hospitals. I administered medications and wept at funerals. Still, even during the toughest times, I thought of myself as one of the lucky ones with enough experience, income, and fortitude to endure what was happening. With age comes wisdom, they say. I am fortunate in many respects, and following my father's last decade, many people tell me I did all the right things.

Really? What is right?

Stories like this one often end with a few upbeat paragraphs summarizing lessons learned. What is it about the story of my father, or the developing ones of Jen or Langer, that might spare others misery? What can an individual actually do to make things better?

I could demur that I know essentially nothing, but that isn't true. After experiencing firsthand the physical and mental decline of so many from AIDS, and now the mental deterioration of three individuals from dementia, I have plenty of thoughts and feelings. I have no solutions but can offer observations constrained—as are physics insights these days— to approximately 4% of the known universe that is dementia.

A mistake I made repeatedly when confronted with an impending crisis was thinking I could handle matters by myself. Jen is doing that right now. Even after professional counsel that a "situation" was beyond my ability to handle, I found it difficult to accede to medical or professional advice and waited too long for outside or in-home help. A principal problem is that I, and many other individuals, tend not to recognize the potentially crushing emotional toll of changing events. In my father's case, I waited too long for a clinical diagnosis, residential care, cancer treatment, and hospice care. I delayed too long before exploring a support group. I was reluctant to discuss issues with other members of the family.

Will Medicare or Medicaid, or some other agency or social network, or perhaps insurance coverage, provide assistance? Experiences differ, but I learned not to bank on anything. You can apply for, then wait months or years for, a Medicaid decision, and ultimately receive little or no compensation. Political climates shift overnight. Actual expenses are greater than expectations: in my father's case the tab was $120,000 for the last year of his life, and only cancer radiation treatment was covered by insurance.

Can a relative or friend lend emotional support? Certainly, especially those who are trusted and have experienced the loss of a loved one. One empathetic confidant is essential, and two or more can do wonders. But people are busy with work and their own lives. Some will care about your problems and a few may offer help, but many will not, or will not help enough to make a difference.

Never argue with a person who has dementia. That much is true, but the advice suggests what *not* to do rather than what *to* do. I learned that changing the subject, joking, or agreeing even when agreement is absurd, is the ticket. Distraction, and doing anything other than disagreeing, is a wise course.

Do plenty of homework when searching for a caregiving facility. Most hospitals and many websites identify certified providers. Monthly fees vary widely, often as a function of zip code and local real estate valuations. Talk with several staff members, other clients familiar with the facility, and do a comprehensive inspection tour.

Hospice experiences and personnel vary greatly. In many areas of the country, there isn't just one hospice in a given county or state, but often several, and different organizations do not hire staff or treat terminally ill people the same way. There will be pain and guilt associated with the loss of a loved one's personality, and then the loss of the person you once knew, no matter what you do, but a hospice can minimize the physical pain associated with dying. To some extent, staff members can help the bereaved as well.

A common observation is that serious illness often takes a toll by compromising individuals in a way that makes them less functional than they were before. Of course people and medical conditions vary, but in the end, I think those with a terminal illness also tend to become *more* of who they were formerly, way down deep. And maybe caregivers do as well. That isn't science, just anecdotal opinion. My soul mate became a kinder individual as his disease progressed. Jen's sense of humor seems to be enhanced. Many others I've known, including my father, became more difficult, even abusive, but then Dad did not know what he was doing and neither did I.

What I know centers on a single word. Emotion. Expect it. Know you can best endure it by staying realistic and healthy. There it is. My 4%.

The Mean in Me-ness

The realization materialized artlessly in my head around the age of five or six. An idea about identity: *I am me.* Rephrased in adult terms, I am the only one to know the me-ness that one day appeared in the world and will one day leave awareness behind.

The impact of identity struck me forcefully and often back then, but it's difficult to summon now the emotional punch it carried. Today, an awareness of me-ness persists but with less awe, perhaps reflecting adulthood. Now other matters trigger a jolt.

What, exactly, is the self within oneself existing as the only entity in the universe to comprehend the sensations, perceptions, and experiences of what it is like to be an individual? A fancy term for the elusive characterization of internal and external knowledge—or justifiable and evidence-based knowing—is epistemology, but that's too broad. Many have described it, the experience of personal identity and self-awareness: Descartes, Locke, Wittgenstein among others. Some neuroscientists would say the experience is universal because humans have a brain able to contemplate itself, though the extent to which anyone other than philosopher–scientists ponder such matters varies from limited to intermittent.

During childhood, grownups described me as cheerful and loud-mouthed, but something changed one morning in the sixth grade when I took the floor to read aloud an assignment. For no obvious reason, I was overcome with physical sensations including shaky hands, dry mouth, thumping heart, and a dread that every eye could penetrate the private physical and emotional aspects of my being. Contemporary psychologists identify the reaction as performance anxiety, and a prescription pill called propranolol provides effective treatment these days, but it was not available back then.

I shot up in height and went lanky, developed acne, wrestled with self-consciousness from head to toe as many teenagers do. In short, I matured from a cute kid to geek whose self-consciousness played a markedly different role than self-discovery.

I liked school, would rather scribble on a blackboard than kick a ball around a field. I entered a private university and joined the same fraternity as my three-year-older brother. Why did those robust and all-round American guys pledge me at all? I was not a "face man." I did not play sports let alone captain athletic teams. I was not socially adept. Short answer: they pledged me because of my brother.

Fraternity life on a private campus with Methodist roots was different then from what it is now. No alcohol was allowed anywhere on university property. Sex-segregated dorms with prim ladies at front desks ensured chastity within. No drugs. No women's groups or gay organizations. No smart phones or laptops or social media because they did not yet exist. And—I was to discover—no blacks accepted into my fraternity. After my sophomore year, I moved out of the frat house not just because of the hazing. Not just because I am gay and was closeted at the time and don't play team sports and our Greek headquarters enforced by charter racial discrimination, but for all those reasons plus a hankering for independence rather than confrontation. I wondered back then if it was the right thing to do. New liaisons confirmed it was.

Today, I wonder why certain people find the borders of their nervous system by imagining trespass and confrontation, by seeing themselves as victims. For example, some of my relatives wear aggressive—dare I suggest, combative—sweatshirts plastered with images of handguns and slogans boasting, "I majored in Triggernometry, so don't tempt me." Why do several of them mount campaigns on social media exclaiming, "You threaten my kid, I'll cut you!" in the absence of threats from anyone? Why are some individuals eager to embrace Confederate flags and related iconography?

Having recently read a nonfiction piece in a first-rate publication (think *The Atlantic* or similar), I asked a couple of far-right relatives to react to the essay's principal contention. The article proposed, in essence, that a huge issue driving conservative thought has to do with an aversion to cheaters. My question was, where on the scale of political importance would the relatives rank, as a problem, people who take advantage of the system? Responses came full-throated, a gradual rising of voices uniting feral testimonials into a barrage of explosive revulsion.

I recall the frustration I felt when pushy kids would cheat in the lunch line at school. We called it "sponging" back then, or cutting line. The behavior was annoying, but would it be possible to reinforce the suggestion that we as adults, and the nation as a whole, have far greater problems than cheaters (i.e., takers) angling for an advantage? Racial and ethnic discrimination for example. Collapsing infrastructures.

Terrestrial and oceanic pollution. Social injustice and the possibility of comprehending our own nature—our me-ness—more fully.

I decided to stick to the economic point by suggesting corporate greed and tax evasion might represent greater abuses than moms who misuse welfare stamps to bring home soda. Or cigs or booze for that matter.

"I think your concern is the U.S. spends about $70 billion annually on the Supplemental Nutrition Assistance Program, which used to be called food stamps?"

"Yes, appalling!"

"Did you know the fossil fuel sector alone gets about $20 billion per year in Federal subsidies? The agricultural sector gets another $25 billion …."

"Lies."

I cite more numbers about colossal losses in Federal revenue courtesy of tax credits for our wealthiest tax-evading citizens and subsidized corporations, amounting to more than $1.3 trillion in tax breaks or roughly 20 times more money than food handouts. I remind family members of the relatively piddly drain on the U.S. Treasury that would accrue from all welfare cheaters, even if they cheated heartily.

Such arguments garnered denial. "No, that isn't true. None of it."

Statistics is a strange bird. Mathematics, it's often said, comes as close as humans are able to the truth, or if not Truth then permanence and validity. Yet statisticians themselves admit numbers can be manipulated to support—or appear to support—almost any thesis. Of late I am convinced that somewhere around 40% of the United States population will believe anything. Absolutely anything. From recent voter outcomes, perhaps the number varies between 30% and 50%, but the point is about gullibility. Did Richard Gere require an emergency gerbilectomy to unclog his butt? Did Hillary Clinton pimp for a child-sex ring operating out of a pizza joint sponsoring satanic rituals? There is nothing—absolutely nothing—people won't believe. Crystals'll disappear you your anxiety, and dinosaurs helped people build them big pyramids over there. Auras and angels hover in the neighborhood of our corporeal essence, and Mexico has a drug that cures cancer. A free press is the enemy of the people, and protestors are thugs or paid socialist agitators. Michele Obama is a man, and political correctness is out to destroy Christmas.

When reality morphs into an enemy and science is scorned, then myths, claptrap, and bunk become truth, and it shocks me. Why does it continue to shock me? Take the old trick of the pot calling the kettle black. In politics especially, accuse one's opponent of your own misdeeds, and people will believe the accusation. The tactic is called projection and features redirection of attention. Incorporate only information that reinforces one's preconceived beliefs, and reject information that contradicts those beliefs. It's called confirmation or "my-side bias" and is related to the idea of cognitive consonance. It feels good and reassuring to have one's personal opinions confirmed. It rankles to ponder alternatives. There is apparently no dopamine or oxytocin high—or substitute here any other flavor of favored neurotransmitter—in second guessing oneself.

Why as a child did I find animal torture aversive while a neighbor kid got a kick out of ripping the legs off frogs and stabbing them through the head with a stick? Was I born with a sense of empathy and compassion? The me-ness inside has an answer. Yes. I was. Was the cruel kid born with a penchant for cruelty? Drawing from nature–nurture tenets, I have to believe in the potency of both genetics and environment.

Nothing is simple, and people can change. People can acquire an appreciation for critical thinking. Yes?

In an era when global information is instantly available on a smart phone, records on rising carbon-dioxide load in the atmosphere are right there for the viewing. Yet about half the U.S. population believes the data are untrue or that humans are not responsible for the numbers.

Here's a theory. Among the powerful forces shaping American society today, two influences are prime: one is a single emotion and the other is an ultimate commodity. The emotion is fear (read, adrenaline), and the commodity is money (the currency of paranoia). Not the garden variety of fear of public speaking, but the kind of fear leading to anger and hatred as white majorities fade into minorities, or terror about being attacked on the street or at home in bed. And not a reasonable and healthy concern with balancing the household budget, but a consuming panic about sinister forces robbing us blind and taking every dollar we have earned. For victimhood and powerlessness, there is no magic bullet, no pill, but there are guns and plenty of monsters at which to aim.

I am no saint, but sometime during childhood my fixation on me-ness expanded and migrated to include the comfort of a pet Cocker Spaniel. It broadened to consider the welfare of parents and grandparents, to the struggles of folks living without access to sufficient food or clean water. Somewhere down the road, I developed an uneasy feeling that self-centeredness can get stuck in people. More than stuck: self-interest can intensify and override other motives. If we asked an individual consumed with fear and hatred, or obsessed with dollars, to work through the implications of solidified self-interest, would the foundation for it break down?

My brother, who lives in the heart of self-fertilizing Rustbelt resentments, is convinced his neighbors' ironclad opinions cannot be changed, no matter the validity of arguments counter to convictions. I argue the opposite in our brotherly conversations, but sometimes find it difficult to sustain enthusiasm because history has something to say about people who embrace elements within an imaginary, closed sphere and distrust what is foreign to it. In today's lingo, the monsters are fingered as cheaters or freeloaders, foreigners or illegals or refugees, the homeless and crazy liberal elites who indulge them. History, with its inevitable dips and hummocks, offers an uneven impression of progress when it comes to accepting the other-minded. Besides, life is boring with Wal-Mart as a principal destination, so why not crank up emotion by conjuring enemies who pay with stamps or speak with foreign accents?

Yet I try to see the landscape through Heartland eyes. Good people anywhere can think right things or wrong things, even stupid things, but strong feelings and absolutism do not imply deep understanding on anyone's part. Good people are entitled to believe other people should stand on their own two feet and work rather than take handouts. It feels right to think such things, and if not exhaustive in implications, then it is not entirely wrong either.

Heartlanders have a point, and if I have a different opinion, can we transcend partisanship? Times are complicated, conclusions seem hazardous, and highly irregular runs the trajectory of human compassion. Space, time, and biology are vast; still, too often we only see the speck that is the *me* in a polymorphous world.

Will and Ariel Durant in *The Lessons of History* (p. 31) offer a conclusion about racial antagonisms, but it applies more generally. "There is no cure for ... antipathies except for a broadened education."[18] Those who credit education in the form of learning and critical thinking are likely to agree, but everyone does not cherish scholarly values, so is there another route to daylight?

If the only genuine emancipation from hatred and ignorance is individual, then a driver for personal change might also need to incorporate individual connectivity. Real, human connection through life-long, nonschool learning—understanding another's perspective without the prerequisite of total agreement—can be sparked through a friend or relative who is gay, a daughter or granddaughter seeking abortion after a physical attack, a neighbor forced into welfare following illness, or a host of other circumstances. Failing education and emotional connectivity, 24-hour hate media fill the void by indoctrinating interpersonal, regional, and national bias entirely counter to appreciating the possibilities inherent in human diversity.

Seeing beyond ourselves through another's reality can help buffer animus. All the not-me's of the world need not mirror me in outlook; however, raising the bar a notch by elevating what might be called the empathy average—or mean in compassionate me-ness—would be a welcome start.

Along the countless paths to self-identity, mine happened to arise spontaneously at an early age, likely through an awakening unease that I was different from the norm. Others might develop a sense of self through ordinary experience, book learning, exposure to diversity, or self-imposed conversion. Even for those who acquire a concept of me-ness late in life, or only vaguely, or in a negative way out of displeasure or shame with who they are, or through hatred of perceived enemies, there remains a positive possibility. If living has anything to do with gaining and losing wisdom, it is also a process in which anyone, everyone, can renegotiate the *me* within. For better or worse—even if assembled on a substrate of granite—me's are formed and reformed.

Three Scenes and the Problem of Intermediate Gray

Scene 1

On an otherwise sunny afternoon around 5 p.m., fog cascading over Twin Peaks dissipates above our 18th Street neighborhood that will find itself mist-shrouded in another hour. For now, in the year 1978, seven of us are comfortable hanging out on a street corner in tee shirts. A hand-rolled joint is making the rounds, and several in our circle tap boots on cement to the beat of a late-70's disco tune emanating from inside Moby Dick, a favored club packed shoulder-to-shoulder with men this hour.

I remind myself today—as before, so many years ago—that I need to remember without embellishment the scene as it unfolds here: a thumping of music along with the rapid beating of hearts. I must mentally reinforce at the ages of 30 or 40 or 50, for more subdued reminiscences in old age and on my deathbed, the underlying character of this experience when it happened. What might be mistaken as self-indulgence is really about affiliation, affection, possible love. I imagine I'm about as happy as a gay person can be anywhere on the planet because my friends and I are free to celebrate in the year 1978 and in this city an emergent luxury of being who we are in public sans sidelong glances of disapproval.

Scene 2

During an eastbound drive on the San Mateo–Hayward Bridge, car tires thump a regular beat atop spaced pavement grids. To the north, high-rise towers defining the downtown business district appear to float the blue horizon above a thin film of water. I'm on my way to work on a weekday morning in the late-1980s, headed for the security gates of a famous National Laboratory in the East Bay where scientists really do model San Francisco Bay as a thin film because it is so shallow. My eyes sting, not from smog or squinting into a sunrise as light reflects off the water, but because later this afternoon, as on other workdays, I will leave my place of employment as a science writer to drive into the city of my dreams for a stop at hospital A, then hospital B, then hospital C to comfort the very-near-death dying.

It must be near the peak of the AIDS epidemic, I imagine from behind the wheel that day, but wonder as well whether there will ever come a "peak," or will it last forever? The first individual I will see as evening falls in the city is one of my closest friends, age 31, whose mother has flown in from Denver to sit with her boy whose body and brain are disintegrating. Dorothy lost her first husband, then a second, and now is bidding farewell to her only child from marriage one. I adore Dorothy for many reasons: foremost is that she has made the effort to show up to be with her boy, unlike many other parents of the HIV-positive. Her no-nonsense realism is marked by an edge of humor when she reminds son Bill of his childhood antics, including the times he would harass unpleasant neighbors by flinging dog turds and orange peels over their back-yard fence, then blame the mess on squirrels.

The sight of downtown city towers had always cheered me from a distance along my commute, but now thoughts of the city bring me low. Who's next? Will everyone I know die of this disease? And the answer I can share—several decades on—is, indeed, virtually every male friend I made in Everyone's Favorite City will die before the twenty-first century dawns, and the total body count by the end of the 1990s will be 330,000 gay men throughout the United States. Exceptions include a friend who flees California to return to celibacy in Michigan and another who drives back "home" to Denver. My soul mate will succumb to cancer just before the Twin Towers collapse, but almost every other city person I befriend on the West Coast—numbering somewhere near a hundred—will die of an eviscerating retrovirus that steals first the flesh of substance, then the mind of mindfulness, until little corporeal or cerebral matter is left to remind a companion or loved one of the person who once was.

Scene 3

My brother and I sit in the newly enlarged living room of our Montana cabin that overlooks jagged peaks of the Livingston Range forming a backbone of Glacier National Park. We have been silent for a while, which makes me grateful for the music from our satellite-connected system out here in the wilderness. I should remind myself of our good fortune in life because I am financially comfortable now, retired and in decent health, and we share a unique vacation retreat where wolves occasionally howl outside the front door. Yet something more unsettling charges the atmosphere.

My brother has just told me during an awkward back-and-forth that I see the world in black and white terms, missing the shades of gray. What I feel in response to the assessment is that my brother takes—or mistakes—my expressed convictions for certainty, and any verbal assertiveness for dogma. I think a learned-response style is at fault for the discomfort between us, but there is also some truth in what he says. I tend to come off as emphatic, verbally aggressive, and sure of myself, a stance adopted in graduate school as a defensive tactic when staking supporting philosophical or psychological claims against detractors. My older brother interprets the style as academic pomposity—certitude—and does not cotton to it.

The truth is I feel uncertain about many things. What I also think, as we sit in the living room of the cabin this evening, is that I wish my brother had been present on one of my swings through San Francisco hospital wards back in the day. Maybe he could understand today another truth had he been witness during even one of my visits at Hospital A or B or C with a dying friend and mother—if a man's mother came to say goodbye—during the worst of the crisis. But he was not there.

Nor was any other member of the family present when I administered morphine to a failing soul-mate, then to my ailing mother who died at the age of 93, or when my father succumbed after a decade-long decline involving vascular dementia. No family was witness when I ushered each of them out of this world and into—for me at least—oblivion, for I do not personally believe in celestial green pastures.

During no fewer than four decades of adult life, it has often felt as though I was placed on earth (metaphor again, because I do not believe in a fateful placement of caregivers) repeatedly to tend the terminally ill pretty much on my own. If some others, perhaps most people, are unable or unwilling to endure the emotional abrasions associated with illness and death, I am apparently made of other stuff.

The Problem

When I was in graduate school completing a degree in neuropsychology, my principal mentor Donald R. Meyer who was a brilliant academic, proposed the same solution any time a student failed to generate an idea with merit for research study. "Image the darkest of all possible blacks and the whitest of all possible whites," the professor would offer. "You will become famous beyond measure and find yourself cited in scores of academic journals," he'd promise, "if you can devise a way to establish that gray that is exactly half way between the blackest black and whitest white." Though the professor was genuinely interested in the neurophysiology of visual discrimination learning, and quantification of an intermediate gray would have useful research applications, I could not help but speculate that the suggestion, which my mentor dubbed "The Problem of the Intermediate Gray," was not entirely devoid of irony.

*

Some people are intrigued by how to fix a car engine or a damaged smartphone. Physical objects of that sort, as well as discovering a hypothetical intermediate gray, do not much interest me. Concepts of fairness, social justice, and compassion do.

Perhaps as a function of my history I really do think in terms of intellectual rights and wrongs—or blacks and whites as my brother puts it—when it comes to human values, while remaining blind to an infinite continuum of grays that others experience. Yet some topics apparently do not suggest an intermediate gray as defensible middle ground. Here is one example. Tell a holocaust survivor you want to rid the word of Jews, and rational discussion can hardly proceed toward some middle ground because rational dialogue never started. It might be reinforcing the obvious to say that I am not a fan of mass murder or hatred, but hold that thought a sec.

Here's another example of an interaction with no apparent position of compromise. Two years ago, my brother's grandson posted on the Internet his desire to "rid the world of fags." In response, I invoked the word "homophobia" in an open letter to my immediate biological tribe who live proximal to the boy and presumably enjoy opportunities for greater influence than I. Some kin labeled me, in turn, judgmental, intolerant, and confrontational because of my reaction: I was the one with the problem here, not the boy. He's just young (a mere 15 at the time) the relatives reasoned; he's naïve and possibly coerced by darker peer influences at school and doesn't mean anything by it; or maybe he's gay himself and needs sympathy. Had I thought of that?

What I thought was the kid might have used the "N" word instead of fag, or another epithet like "cunt" or "those heathen Muslims," and his unhappy sentiment would remain squarely at home in the annals of hatred.

Several years hence, the only developments to report on the family's fag-extermination front—pro or con—is my brother's suggestion that I see only black and white, and harbor "unresolved issues." If so, one of the issues might entail hiring a hit man to trim someone's toenails, so to speak, though my revenge circuitry only functions in ideational mode.

Why do I go on and on about something that happened a few years ago? What am I really thinking? While my more reasoned perspective on the topic of "ridding the world of (insert any brand of human being)" remains black and white, I want to see the intermediate gray in various arguments out there in less-liberal terrain beyond the golden hills of loopy-left-wing Berkeley and San Francisco, California, but I could be sun-blinded by memories of an urban atmosphere on those weekend afternoons when I hung out with pals—among the finest people I've known—who are no longer around to encourage me to dance and smile. I want to ponder nuances in various arguments regarding right- or left-handed causes but remain tone-deafened by 70s and 80s disco tunes celebrating wild release as the guys and I sweated our corporeal essences on dance floors in certain locales around a nation newly offering to us, or at least not criminalizing any longer, expressions of personal freedom. I want to think kindly of mild-mannered true believers in rural America who "mean no harm" and yearn for a return to those better days, those great days, in a land they once respected and loved, where people knew their roles and places in life—at least straight white males did. However, I remain sensitized by nightmare recollections of the wasted torsos and oozing brain fluids of so many individuals—doctors and dentists and decorators, carpenters and cooks and kooks—too young justifiably to depart this vale of tears. Not only too young to die as they did but accompanied by political blindness and denial, by fear and hatred; or by some presumptive and imagined certainty regarding what it is that constitutes proper versus improper sexual expression; or to the tune of sermons invoking some intermediate but self-righteous shade of belief centered on the idea that "it says so right here" in a favored religious scripture.

Why can't I just be quiet? More than one relative asks: why can't I just let it go and move on? What good does confrontation do?

The better part of me advises another part—the troubled part, the furious part—to avoid the petty jabs of uncomprehending minds. Still, when I reflect on my nephew's expressed goal in life and some family members' reaction to it, I am reminded of iconic venues, including Auschwitz–Berkenau in the 1940s and Everyone's Favorite City during and after the 1970s. I am haunted by those jewel-like Sunday afternoons at social clubs lining 18th Street and the flutter of a dozen rainbow flags hung from lampposts in the Castro District, of a hundred thump-a-thumping disco tunes and the wretched purple lesions signaling an onset of Kaposi's sarcoma and doom on the flesh of folks I once embraced in friendship or romance, and of a thousand sunsets out at the Golden Gate where ten thousand souls bridging flesh tones from the blackest of black to the whitest of white once experienced camaraderie and liberation, but will experience neither any more.

Oh, those wild afternoons and subdued, imagined tomorrows. Black, white, and gray be damned. I think the real story must lie in the infinite coloration of those times—don't you?—in the uniquely human experiences and stories of the dead my young nephew need never fear he might be required to hear.

Listen, I want to say. Listen to them all. But no, because they have gone silent.

Never At Home At Home

Don't say, "I don't know what you mean," when you mean something else. No one is deceived when the message is code for avoidance.

I used to socialize with dozens of people. Scores. We'd meet in the city every weekend to swap the melodies of our private lives, boogie afternoons into sunset, then breathe nocturnal aromas into dawn. We rejoiced in an illusory freedom from institutional and legal judgment, unshackled, we supposed, from the faith we'd given away to others who needed to believe in something at the expense of someone else. We were mistaken.

We were hundreds, thousands before the premature jubilance was overtaken by physical afflictions only a few survived. Several fell weekly at the outset, more than a hundred the first year. Hundreds of thousands eventually succumbed in the U.S. alone, many with only a small section of patchwork quilt for a tombstone to commemorate second deaths. I'm talking about those who died a little at first on the inside of emotional alienation, then again from religious condemnation, quack "therapy," or plain old bigotry. You know the ones: the pasty boys who were egged in alleys or stabbed or shot in broad daylight or strung up on barbed wire; the swish or fem or shy disowned by moms and pops across Middle America; the macho men or bodies beautiful or leather guys who scoffed at narrow-mindedness only to die both inside and out during a plague witnessed by the world and reinforced through political denial because, after all, who cares about some social–sexual deviants?

If you say, "I don't know what you mean," or, "I don't know what you're talking about," or, "No one can possibly understand what others lived through back then," I hear the words as something else. Culture the verbal denials I've encountered over the years and incubate for truth, and the results reveal themselves as false positives. "I don't know what you mean" might imply disagreement, as in: I don't want to discuss it further because you're wrong in your thinking. Or it could mean I don't care and never will. It could mean I wasn't there and don't know much about it, or we live in such different worlds we'll never understand each other. But don't say, "I don't know what you mean," to suspend the possibility of dialog in casual dismissal.

When I say *now*, I mean the vogue of shrugging memory loss. When

I say *then*, I mean how life experiences construct an individual's truth. This is what I mean. We were Turkish or Irish or Spanish in origin, African and Australian and Asian, every flavor of devout or secular. We were mostly in our 20s and 30s, and we usually lived and worked and loved in urban locations. We loved, that is, until skin and muscle and brain tissue unexpectedly seized before withering from an affliction so righteously viral in selective desiccation that a leader of the free world at the time dared not speak its name.

Can you predict from once-flawless skin all a youth might have become? Do you know how far someone's hands might have extended the curative power of mercy to counter injustice, had they lived? These were the days of *then*, them versus us, deniers against a dying breed, and each time another of us died, part of me died as well.

It's tempting to dismiss a man who's lost patience with *now* because of *then*, and doesn't cotton to rationalizations. But instead of crooning a tune about job or financial insecurities in the modern era, the era of alternative truths, of fake pandemics, and don't-tread-on-me, tell me instead what you understand about endings. While you're at it, forget the notion there's something in this world called karma, because there isn't. Full stop.

What you want, of course, is for people to forgive and forget. But remember: you might not realize how much you love someone—or someone loves you in return—until the person's consciousness vanishes on some plague-filled afternoon.

The modern-day disease-spreaders keep coming at me now, so let me remind you. Every time I start something, there they are again. If they keep calling and knocking, I will not be responsible, so I yell at them, "Go away. I'm not at home. Nobody's here," but they keep knocking or ringing or popping up on television and social media. It's not nice to label someone a disease-spreader, is it?

Everybody plans for the future, thinking about grand times ahead or just down the road. The disease-spreaders have their minds entirely on the future, with their boxed cookies and canned speeches and good-news pamphlets preaching faith everlasting in the current currency. They look forward to a brighter tomorrow beginning tomorrow, a happy tomorrow filled with prosperity and greatness and spiritual fulfillment, or even just another tomorrow like today, starting tomorrow if only we will believe. What they suck at is planning for a crap tomorrow, the one with endings where everyone you ever knew and loved lies under a quilted headstone. You know, a tomorrow like the one that happened yesterday and that is actually going to happen to every one of us in the end. A tomorrow as in reality. We stink at planning for that kind of tomorrow. Joan Didion said something like that somewhere or other, and she was right. Everybody loves beginnings—another baby and a new car with that new baby and new car smell—never thinking about the heap on which everything ends up being tossed, babies and lovers included.

Is that too bitter? Am I a fool, or is there a reason I sound angry and keep repeating myself?

You want everyone to be like you rather than to think as I think and remember what I remember. But the truth is every time I hear the righteous pamphlet hawkers and faith dispensers talk, I can feel my IQ plummet from atmospheric ignorance. What I hear is the same story from individuals—much like holocaust deniers—and an entire society that doesn't know enough to plan for an honest-to-god tomorrow. They're sweet and hopeful though, right? The pamphlet and boobtube and cookie kids are sweet like hard candy, but with an intellectual core of denial that'll rot all the teeth in your head.

Maybe you've gathered I never believed in providence or pyramid power, in a god of vengeance and mercy, in the dichotomy of right and left hemispheres, in the gastrointestinal value of gluten-freedom or my bio-superiority. If all those things are nonsense to me, let me share instead something that's true, then maybe you'll hear the truth in what I mean. It's about a physical place in mental space, but it's truer than anything else I ever knew.

Listen. Please.

Imagine you embark on a road trip into the Gallatin Canyon along a highway that clips the northwest corner of Yellowstone Park. Or imagine my taking that drive before the ones I knew and loved were gone, and before I understood who I was. If you haven't been out to that Western territory of the United States, you won't understand what the country is like, and I can't do justice to the terrain by describing it in words. It's a real place you have to see for yourself and breathe in and out to allow the essence to penetrate the brain. The air. The pine and spruce growing there. As if everyone a person ever knew were still alive and well. It's a big horizon embroidered below by white-flecked streams alive with the living and echoes of the dead. Alive with the potential of who you really are as a person.

See? I can only use words here, and words can't do it justice. But let's keep trying anyway.

I looked over my shoulder while driving that road the first time one autumn afternoon, and there it was. A dirt lane leading to a place set back from the highway, and I was certain. I knew I belonged there more than any other place. Belonging has nothing to do with ownership, by the way, nothing to do with money or ancestry or orientation. The feeling of belonging there among the trees and streams was overwhelming and never left me. It remains as powerful now and indisputable as the day I first saw the place. It's nothing like the disease-spreaders around here who want to step into my life and give it "meaning," if I would only let them in. The place I'm describing is real to me in a personal sense. How real?

I'm in that pine and spruce terrain in my brain every time I think about it. It has nothing to do with a decision or time. Or, rather, it transcends time. I'm in yesterday's windstorm with the gusts scraping twigs along an outside wall of the ranch house. I'm in the way the pine and spruce and wind call my bones and address something central in me. Something that *is* me. And if I can feel so enraptured by an image and captivated by a sideways glance, then I wonder: what else have I missed in life? Life itself? The genuine article?

I am the leaves piled in a corner the wood-rail fence makes with that ranch house. If you turn my leaves over, the damp underneath is the slight of old wounds left behind. Remember, I know something about wounds, the dead, and dying. Some part of me has always been there and is there now.

Down deeper still, under the damp, lay the rot of last year, a season my better counselors tell me it's best to let go, as if letting go of memory and feeling fertilizes the soil underneath to encourage my new growth. Just let it all go, folks try to tell me, to sprout new branches that will touch the eaves and scrape the outside wall of the ranch house in the wind for some future me standing inside to hear. A future me that was once possible. As if the place harbored curative spirits, and every time I hear the sound of wind in the branches, or imagine it, I am at home in the place I knew before seeing it. It is my place. The only place I ever understood for the life I wanted to live. Discovering the place was like being born while alive and given a chance at genuine life.

It's real, is what I want to say to you. It's both a real place and a metaphor for the real me that once was possible when the light still shone for me on some possible tomorrow. It's the genuine article. You don't have to like the place, my place. You don't have to approve. I'm not an estate agent trying to sell you property or a state of mind, but what you can't do is dismiss a place as wrong for someone else because it isn't right for you.

I walk up to the front door, and someone I've always known opens it wide. I'm in the past of that place with its pine and spruce climbing the vertical mountains behind the corral; I'm in the present logs and future decay that will return to nature my nature. I belong in that place in my head and heart every day of my life and with every part of my body, and discover there's a word for it. The word is authenticity. Authenticity. It's a physical place. It's an emotional place. I *am* that place, the me that once might have been before the world insisted my nature was mistaken.

Now I'll tell you something else. Years later, I drove that road again, alone, longing for the place in the wild mountains, but finding it was not there. Which is the way the future lets a person down, the way time works. The way leaving a piece of yourself behind and a part uninhabited, along with those departed, sometimes means you can never get it back. If you miss such things in life, they're gone.

If you still say, "I don't know what you mean; I don't know what you're talking about," I can only answer that maybe you don't know because you won't allow yourself to feel what I feel. You were not there when we danced and sang, I know, I understand, and if what I'm describing now still means nothing to you, maybe you aren't really present, listening. Are you listening?

Blame me if you will because I make you uncomfortable. Or pretend it's all so much better nowadays, and the injustice and ignorance that wiped millions of souls from the planet happened way back a long time ago, and it's not like that anymore. And it's not your fault. And you didn't do it. Or pretend a magical future will improve upon the present to make it great.

Right there: that's the problem. Magical thinking about how our problems can disappear given enough time and by tossing some good will or money at a cause.

On top of that, I'm the lucky one because I survived. Right? So get over it and move on, right?

Here's what I can do. In my head even now, as late as it is, I can walk in that conceptual forest of lodgepole pine and Engelmann spruce where streams trickle down the mountain canyons and dance past a ranch house. I can breathe in air where *imagination is everything,* as Einstein put it once, and inside my head and body, I am that place. Genuine and whole as I might once have been and remained. Being myself.

You can decide there are two types of people in this world: the true-believers and the grumps out there, essentially the young and old, the upbeat versus cantankerous pessimists. But I say there are as many types as there are dreams and as many dreams as people who aren't dead inside, and in my head, I can return to the trees and wind and be alive again.

Now, I wait for my metaphorical tray of powdered milk and Pablum. I hear the door to my room being locked every night by thoughtful and protective caregivers. It's the same metallic click every night to keep me safe from myself. Or so some suppose. *Click.* Do you hear it? It's right there in my future and in yours.

It's the same sad click I recall from childhood. Of playground exclusion and familial denial, the click of worshipers locking gates around their church of intolerance, thoughts into the minds of family-value voters, hopelessness inside the doors of county jail cells and psychiatric wards.

I close my eyes and return to those woods and am free to realize a vision of being complete at last. Of being myself. Now, when everything and everyone else I ever knew are gone, when it's dead quiet around me and no one is banging on my skin and the phone isn't ringing and breaking news isn't blaring, I close my eyes and inhabit a terrain where I cannot live too slowly.

I live slowly then, slowly, breathing in and out a final recollection on behalf of all the ones I knew or loved who never got to live and breathe what they might have been. Instead of the anger you think you hear me casting into the air tonight, might it be a song of mourning for so many lives?

Move on; forgive and forget, I keep hearing people say, and my answer is yes. And no. Yes to the genuine. No, never forget. Just don't say it to me again. Don't say, "I don't know what you mean."

Author's Note:

(The following statement—requested and printed by the journal first publishing "Never At Home At Home"—provides some clarification about my reasons for writing this essay.)

At a relatively young age, I'd lost more friends and acquaintances than some people know over the course of a lifetime. This hybrid story is principally nonfiction seasoned with surreal imagery intentionally evocative and vexing. Rather than mere venting, the essay is a challenge to individuals with edited memories—or, worse, ignorance—about events only a few decades ago. Surviving a tragedy that cut short the lives of an estimated 330,000 gay men in the U.S. according the CDC[63] and 32 million humans around the globe[64] also arouses in me what feels like an obligation to the silenced, and in the recent political climate, a responsibility to remind our better selves about a fraught past. I want to say, "Understand, please, our recent history," especially in the context of ongoing expressions of social disapproval and partisan antagonism aimed at "those people" (immigrants, minorities, the disenfranchised, the LGBTQ cohort, and many others) who remain outside some mythical, mainstream "us." Is the essay choleric, and is acrimony warranted? Yes, on both counts. A remedy then? One avenue suggested here is to recognize individual authenticity versus its absence, the latter often manifest as witlessness and self-deception riling those within and beyond our immediate purview.

Repeating Their Names

Everyone will face the ultimate reality, but in the meantime, some prefer to avoid thinking about inevitabilities while others make a show of bravado or arrogance. Each reaction, including abjuration, reveals something about character.

The departed, deceased, the lost. Six feet under and resting in peace, or pushing up daisies in a better place. In a more wishful and self-indulgent vein, "the transitioned" serves as trendy lingo, but regardless of the cliché—morbid, humorous, or palliative—death is the inevitable destination for everyone alive and increasingly germane with advancing age.

At this point in the journey, I envision a monumental balance scale with all the individuals formerly near and dear to my heart outnumbering and, in an emotional sense, out-weighing those people still breathing and central to my existence because, I fear, I sometimes take the latter for granted. It would be pleasant to imagine those whose life-force has "slipped away" as luxuriating, weightless and unburdened, in green pastures, but I put even less stock in happy-ever-after imagery than in bravado.

Euphemisms and personal beliefs aside, this morning a friend called to lament the sudden and crushing loss of his personal buddy and colleague of 40 years. Although I knew it wasn't feasible to banish my friend's immediate pain conversationally with a few remarks after such an emotional forfeiture, I wanted to offer my caller something, so I described a private ritual.

To acknowledge each of the dearly and permanently departed from my life, I've developed a routine every morning while hiking a trail up and down a ridge behind my house. A round trip takes about an hour to complete and includes two modest hills: up sharply, then down gently, up and down again before the gradual incline back home. Were I to select an eastern fork along the pathway, I could head as far as 20 miles up and up into remote regional parkland where song birds, a variety of raptors, and coyotes would be my only likely companions. I've walked some of the longer trails, but that alternative is not a regular choice because—at my age again—I know if I set myself an arduous task, chances are excellent I'll delay and delay. The probability of tackling a relatively brief undertaking remains good these days, but not if the mental preparation or physical effort is daunting.

A key concept here again is age. I've developed a few techniques at this point in life to come to terms with the loss of those who will remain absent from physical purview forevermore. My approach involves walking and reflecting in a specific way.

As I conquer the hills before the California sun gets too intense, I say their names and sometimes wonder, walking and repeating the names of the dead—aloud or to myself—why I say them, knowing the answer is difficult to articulate. Meanwhile, over there, off to one side of the path just now is a coyote pup, then another, and then a third. With more interesting natural features to draw their attention than a lone human mumbling to himself, the pups do not hear me say the names. A falcon rises on a current of air above this ridge, locally known as Falcon Ridge, as I watch the young coyotes chase each other and tumble, like some of my named friends and lovers once tumbled, long ago or more recently, into and out of my rooms or I into theirs. I watch the falcon soar on updrafts just as we—the named departed and I—once navigated emotional currents on a foggy or sunny afternoon in a San Francisco museum for art's sake, or through coastal twilight conversations for the mind's sake, or into enfolding arms for comfort's sake.

The coyote pups disappear from view, like so many friends and family members, now numbering dozens and dozens, who once knew some key part of me while they lived. So I say their names again, one after another, slowly and mostly to myself to acknowledge what they knew of me and to keep thoughts of them alive in the world, if only momentarily, as I would want those who know me now to keep active a trace of my existence after I am no more. At least for a while.

Can some intentional or extended contemplation of death reduce the fear of dying? A few gurus-for-profit answer in the affirmative, but I'm not so sure.

I say the names simply to honor the departed, to acknowledge what the dead once meant and still mean to me. I say the names to chart my advance along life's inevitable living-to-dying progression, to give a nod to both mortality and my good fortune in remaining here on earth in good health today while so many others are gone from the world I knew. I repeat the names to counter the weight of silence and loss by reminding myself to make some contribution to the world. Saying the names is about mortality then, but it's also about the temporariness of everything in the world. It has to do with answering difficult questions, like what am I doing today? What am I leaving behind that has value to anyone? It's about reminding myself to contribute something, while understanding the dead can no longer actively participate, and everything is temporary. I say the names to address the idea of a personal legacy, given the certainty and proximity of my own demise, though I have no facile answer about what form a legacy should take. I say the names to caution myself, knowing the job in life at least for me is not so much to win, but to learn.

Today on the nature trail, I remember again the men I knew then loved or loved then knew, and the women, often kinder than the men now departed. About the ones I loved and lost, there comes an undying feeling inadequately characterized as heartache. It's a word I did not appreciate in childhood until I first experienced a hollow, emotional throb after the loss of a treasured pet. Then an uncle died, and a few uncomfortable thoughts kept recurring spontaneously: hazy images of months and years ahead without my uncle dropping by for dinner. How it was that my uncle who loved cars would never experience next year's model of automobiles, and next year and the next.

But why so much fuss about the dead? Dangerous to hold grief in, I suspect, but impossible to shut it out. Or when grief evolves into something else, a muted sadness just behind memory, never possible to describe fully, the need remains to hold it in or out, closer or away, to suppress or monumentalize absence and longing in some manner that is personal and meaningful. But in the end, the reason to contemplate death and the dead is beyond words because it's about coping with something beyond reach.

Still, I want to learn how to die. If that sounds morbid, it doesn't diminish the curiosity. With a graduate degree in what used to be called physiological psychology in the academic world (now labeled neuropsychology), no one need remind me dying is not a process requiring practice. I've watched death happen so many times, and with such varying degrees of quietude or distress, not to understand dying is a biological process rather than a learned behavior. Still, like playing the piano or driving a car or learning German, something inside urges me to figure out the process beforehand so I can avoid making a mess of things. Is it possible not to make a mess, for the sake of others, of dying?

From all those deaths observed over the years, a common thread emerges in my head about the process itself of dying. How individuals die often mirrors and accentuates personality characteristics evident during life. So many times, I've watched unhappy people become increasingly unhappy, angry individuals more enraged, and kind people more humane and generous toward the end.

One thing I do know is that death, real death by natural causes, has little to do with images on a flat or giant silver screen. Death is rarely a fade-out but more often slow music sung in a language that cannot be taught (though I want to learn it), and danced by a body failing to keep the beat. Dying, that effluvial dance macabre, too often expresses itself as a gradual falling away of flesh from bone, an intrusive, graceless, odiferous, sometimes noisy and inevitably noisome affair that shows respect for neither the dying nor those who care about them.

Before the AIDS decades, I understood dying mostly as an abstraction. One relative is said to have taken a bullet on a foreign battlefield, and a maternal grandfather died of cirrhosis in a VA hospital, but those were things I'd heard described by my parents rather than experienced first-hand. As a tyke I'd had a glimpse of a casket at a funeral home, but not what was left of my paternal grandfather who lay inside. I was told another relative had perished halfway across the country in a big city, but the image amounted to little more than a blur. With AIDS and the loss of most West Coast personal friends at the time, the process of experiencing dying was protracted and repeated over the course of two decades, and excruciatingly personal.

Old folks die, and we feel abandoned, but we understand it's the way nature works. Or so we tell ourselves. People we care for in their prime are taken away, and we are lost.

From the death of so many friends, and the loss of a soulmate to cancer as well, I discovered something unexpected in myself. It is often the people professing to care most deeply who end up avoiding the dying. Then again, who can blame them? Ignorance is not bliss but often is preferable to a horrible truth. My soulmate knew many people who claimed to care about him, but of the numerous friends, nearly all shied away at the end from a pain they could not face. I found I was not cut of the same cloth. He lived many months longer than physicians predicted and died in his own bed under the care of two people: me and one other, a genuine friend defined by voluntary actions rather than words.

His passing left me with an awareness of two distinct minds within a single body, one rational and one emotional. The rational part whispers that an inevitable death is preferable to suffering, whereas the sentimental aspect rips my heart apart to this day. Some mornings I awaken from a recurring dream we are together again, before the anguished return to awareness. The rational does not converse much with the emotional: such is the duality of contemplation on the occasion of death.

Of course there are no pat answers about how an individual *should* respond to death, rather, perhaps as many ways to cope or fail to cope with impending or permanent loss as there are humans still alive and lucid. The mechanisms include avoidance, denial, repression, resentfulness, resignation, humor, and acceptance, among other stages of grief formulated by the Swiss–American psychiatrist Elizabeth Kübler–Ross. Many individuals simply do not know what to do or say, as with those who vanished after learning about the diagnosis of my soulmate. But if the inner world, of which death is a part, is as significant as the external, then dodging reality may be the more emotionally damaging option. In troubled and troubling times, unresolved grief issues add to personal burdens. Trying to heal a wound that never heals can also be a source of inspiration, as is apparent when reading writers such as Tony Morrison and James Baldwin.

Through many reminders of the past rushing headlong in my direction, I try to think of the present more than the future these days, believing a measure of wisdom comes with appreciating what is happening in the here and now. Right here. Right now. Yet as much is revealed by how we respond to what has happened during a lifetime. In the end, meaning and insight—if we are lucky—reveal themselves through context and a retrospective appreciation of the flow of events. In the end, it can be as much about what we didn't do as what we did, who we did not love, or what we did not say as opposed to what we expressed. We are what we've done and where we are now, but we are also what remains of unrealized dreams and expressions as we advance into the history of our lives.

Repeat the names of those you've lost to see if the exercise does something for the named or for you, or find your own process, because being mortal but wanting to touch immortality, in death we become our admirers through whom some part of us might live on at least for a while. Maybe we can rediscover part of ourselves as well, momentarily, in the dwindling space between our life and death.

It All Comes At You

For much of the 20th century, "mind" was regarded by most hardcore neuroscientists as a dirty word: a sloppy expression—mystical and unscientific—and a vague metaphor for what goes on inside our heads. More recently the notion of mind has been reinterpreted by some, the clinical neurologist Oliver Sacks[65] among them, as not only a legitimate subject of scientific research but at the center of everything that makes us human, and possibly *the* big problem awaiting elucidation in the next era. We humans are mindful—more and less—as we experience the world, and some dare to suggest certain animals might be mindful too.

In lieu of resolving what mind does and does not include, and assuming by mindful we mean something akin to thoughtful awareness, some other concepts are useful. Consciousness. Attention. Consolidation. Psychologists chart the different states of wakeful experience on a slippery scale of human awareness leading to the possibility of being (in social-justice slang) "woke." But where, when, and exactly how in the brain do we know what's going on? Details about what constitutes the biological basis of mind—or even awareness—are immensely complicated, the objects of study are elusive targets, and definitions of terms resist easy answers.

Think visually then. If consciousness is ambient light, attention aims a focused laser to guide information and comprehension into secure, long-term memory centers of the brain for a "stamping in" process dubbed consolidation. Or think neuroscience. The brains of brain un-teasers chart wakeful brain states through chemical and electrical currents to a hopeful shore. The ultimate dock is the next big thing in understanding what it really means to be mindful, and in our daily lives the possibility of prediction and control.

So much for theory. What we experience every day in the real world is—well—reality, isn't it?

Sometimes we see things clearly, believing what inhabits the mind's eye at the moment must be true. Then again, mental images flicker, come and go, yielding inconsistent snapshots of an inconstant world tinted by belief.

Sometimes we say things unambiguously, imagining our words are understood. More often, communication miscarries, creating reflections of light and sound that intersect with a shared stream of consciousness in an expanding universe.

A relative steers into a skid and fumes invectives when his child is called out for bullying. A teacher banishes an irksome boy to reform school for a contrived offense while a girl comes at you with a fork. A mother packs the car and flees with her daughter while another teenager spurned by family and community finds currency in urban alleyways. It all comes at you that way out of the blue, unconsolidated sky.

Your candidate wins election the week the sky turns orange. Intellectually barren, scientifically illiterate, and morally bankrupt policymakers render politics tribal and toxic. For decades, blood runs red, white, and blue on city streets where walls explode intermittently in flames and boundaries are fortified. Paranoid neighbors shrink behind locked doors safeguarding closets packed with ammo. Meanwhile and with renewed if temporary buoyancy, we are discharged tumor-free and handed an envelope containing a bill for $178,000 on which a single aspirin is listed at $148.62. It isn't the *aspirin*, they explain. Are we paying attention yet in the half-light of nonlinear living?

Or this. On a warm day, we meet as friends sharing thoughts by a river when the sounding forest begins to lose the brightness of afternoon, and we ask a question—

"Did you ever lie to yourself about something you can't admit?"

—and two possibilities come to light.

The first is a bugbear just over the shoulder and everywhere we go. It would scare the bejesus out of a warrior, and its name is fear. The second possibility often arising from the first takes various forms. Self-deception, bias, prejudice, dogmatism, chauvinism, bigotry, jingoism, misogyny, intolerance, hatred, and other comportments we become adept at denying while deploying.

Years on, we wonder what it might have been like. To have a day back, that day at the river. When we were mindful, conscious despite self-consciousness. Attentive, we imagined. In the presence all along of unconsolidated good and evil we did not fully comprehend.

Concluding Thoughts

Sense and nonsense, insight and foolishness, we like to think we live on the bright side of rationality. Distinctions and contradictions between what we think and the real world have been a topic of interest to people from P.T. Barnum, the circus owner and expert manipulator, to the philosopher Ludwig Wittgenstein. The chapters of this book—free ranging in aspect and gravity—are largely concerned with tensions among thought, fantasy, and reality. In the end, words, thoughts, and opinions we hold dear and defend with passion are often as weakly constructed as a diaphanous fabric woven from insubstantial belief.

For many years, my brother and I have taken polar positions on the question of whether it's possible to change minds about emotionally loaded topics, especially if the roots of belief are political or religious in nature. When teaching psychology, I advised introductory students that psychology is the science of understanding, explaining, predicting, and controlling behavior. Understanding in the context of human psychology roughly means being aware and perceptive of a given behavior, explaining is the ability to describe some underlying variables related to the behavior, predicting is about foretelling behavior before it happens, and controlling—the most challenging of the four objectives—means being able to regulate behavior in some way, especially when it interferes destructively with daily life. Given my chosen specialty and at least this somewhat arbitrary definition of psychology, I took the predictable position with my brother that even entrenched human behaviors can be modified, else what is the point of psychology and psychologists? My brother, who still resides in the conservative, rural Midwest where we both grew up, argues beliefs—especially those of an extreme political or spiritual nature among locals—are not amenable to change, and he has become more convinced of his conclusion over the years.

For the last decade or so, human affairs in the U.S. and around the world have taken a turn I could not have predicted as a college freshman reading Orwell's dystopian *1984* and Huxley's prophetic *Brave New World*. Back in school, I felt sure such chilling visions of human affairs, both disturbing and arguably insightful, were also unrealistic because they could not become real in the real world. Then when outlets like Breitbart and Fox News came along, proclamations as apparently absurd or counterintuitive as those in Orwell or Huxley seemed to strike welcoming cords among audiences. Suddenly the press was the enemy, and news from standard media sources was fake, except for the odd Hilary–pizzagate, child-prostitution scandal. Politicized "breaking-news" stories have been increasingly interspersed in recent years with denials regarding climate change, attacks on the value of science, and general accusations of intellectual elitism directed at those holding academic degrees. Other outlets, including MSNBC have been perhaps less strident but no less emphatic in enumerating atrocities associated with political opponents. Today, conspiracy theories are so in-your-face on broadcast news and social media—and indeed around the world, from the UK and Hungary to Brazil—that they diminish the likelihood of productive dialogue among folks favoring flags of one color or another.

There is nothing particularly new here. Back in 1995, the astrophysicist and author Carl Sagan wondered in *The Demon-Haunted World,* how uncritical thinking and anti-intellectualism in general can be addressed.[66] How is it possible to counter those who make up stuff merely to be seen as right, or to gain some political or power advantage, with no regard or outright distain for what is verifiable? In his chapter, "The Fine Art of Baloney Detection," Sagan identifies several cognitive tools and techniques well worth reiterating to protect against falsehoods. A short list includes the following ideas:

1. Seek independent confirmation of facts.
2. Debate evidence by knowledgeable proponents of all points of view.
3. Understand there are experts, but none whose views cannot be questioned.
4. Consider more than one hypothesis, then think of tests to disprove each. What survives has a better chance of being the right answer.
5. Don't get attached to a hypothesis just because it's yours.
6. Quantify what can be quantified.
7. Insist on a chain of argument where every link in the chain must work.
8. Apply Occam's Razor: given two hypotheses to explain data, choose the simpler.
9. Ask if the hypothesis can, in principle, be falsified. Untestable, unfalsifiable propositions are not worth much.

Another aspect of Sagan's baloney-detection system centers on ways to avoid common fallacies of logic and failures of common sense. Among the most noteworthy and commonly encountered errors in logic to be avoided are:

1. *Ad hominem* argument: attacking the arguer rather than addressing the argument.
2. Authority: trusting a person or idea only because the individual or concept is presumably authoritative (similar to #3, above).
3. Appeal to ignorance: what has not been proven false must be true, or vice versa.
4. Begging the question: assuming something without independent evidence.
5. Failing to understand statistics, for example, the null hypothesis or *p* value.
6. *Non sequitur* fallacy: the pretense that something will follow, without evidence.
7. *Post hoc, ergo propter hoc*: mistakenly thinking something happening next was caused by something happening earlier just because of the time sequence.
8. False dichotomy: considering only extreme, but not intermediate, cases.
9. Confusing correlation and causation. Correlation does not prove a causal relation.
10. Straw-man argument: caricaturing a position falsely to attack it more easily.

I still think the four goals of psychology are achievable and that it is possible to change the minds of individuals, but I've made a concession to my brother's point of view. Some folks who are otherwise unremarkable appear to be almost entirely resistant to rational argument and logic. I have known people who believe there is absolutely no difference between fact and opinion, therefore all things—including documented historical events and arithmetic—are merely personal opinion. In the case of entrenched anti-intellectualism, I concede the point to my brother that perhaps it is useless to engage such people in debate. Recall from "The Confidence Paradox" chapter of this book that even the poorest-performing students in the Dunning–Kruger experiments, who were subsequently shown capable of making measurable improvements in judgement and critical thinking, were already enrolled in college and apparently valued education. If a person does not value learning, then opportunities for rational discussion may be futile.

As far back as when I attended grade school, it seemed to me humanity faced an obstacle so daunting that the notion of bringing more children into the world amounted to foolishness. The evidence to me was everywhere apparent: in packed classrooms and on crowded highways, in shops and theatres, spurring every war around the globe and underlying many forms of human misery, from famine and plague to poverty. How was it possible others did not see what I could see? The root cause of so many ills troubling mankind—I believed as a kid and still do to this day—is overpopulation. Today much or little is made of climate change and global warming while the gross domestic product (GDP) is offered as a value or index that can increase without end. Scientists warn the world is running dangerously short of fresh water as aquifers around the world are depleted to grow surpluses of human food often left to rot, even as sea levels rise to inundate cities and entire countries with salt water. Fossil fuels are a vanishing commodity as the global human population has increased three-fold, according to international databases, from 2.5 to about 8 billion since my days of grade-school speculation. *Homo sapiens* are widely regarded as the intelligent ape, so how can a species be so wise yet oblivious of facts?

Beyond the "population bomb" first characterized by Paul Ehrlich[67] decades ago and all the logical-reasoning pitfalls eloquently described by Carl Sagan, it seems to me five additional obstacles handicap reasoned exchange and are root causes of many human misunderstandings. The roadblocks to rational assessment and dialogue are magical thinking, politicization, powerlessness, victimization, and a misunderstanding of science.

Magical thinking is a belief that some event happens as a result of another without any link or causation between the two, despite evidence to the contrary. The saying, "step on a crack: break your mother's back," captures the idea. Similarly, magical thinking can refer to a belief that some circumstance entirely unrelated to a course of events influences an outcome. Lucky charms, knocking wood, angels, karma, and the like are examples of human fabrications to account for, or guard against, the seemingly unaccountable. Through magical thinking, anything can cause anything, or something can happen with no cause whatsoever. The outcomes of such thinking include irrational behavior and making extraordinarily bad choices. For example, we might ignore or disdain overwhelming scientific evidence that mankind is changing the earth and its climate in directly observable and predictably catastrophic ways. Other undesirable outcomes include arguably naïve opinions that the world is a miraculous place that can take care of itself regardless of human actions or inaction, or, if it is not capable of doing so, then ignorance is bliss.

By politicization, in a negative and partisan sense, I mean imposing a political character on some issue that is not inherently political. Consider the nature of love, hurricanes, curtains, disease, or vegetables. At first thought, there is no obvious reason to interpret such items or events in political terms, and the same might be said of topics such as abortion and the COVID-19 pandemic. Why then have some concepts become heavily politicized in today's culture while others have not? The answer is that politicization usually occurs when a topic can be recast to the advantage or disadvantage of a given political or financial entity. When does an adult, in collaboration with an attending physician who has sanctioned medical expertise, not have the right to be in control of his or her own body? Answer: when that right is usurped by politicians, insurance companies, or other invested parties who generally have no medical expertise, but heavy financial or religious stakes in issues like end-of-life suicide, birth control, or abortion, among others.

As another clear example of politicization, there is nothing intrinsically political about a virus that has evolved on earth over an estimated 1.5 billion years.[68] Furthermore, if anything can be said about the "purpose" of a virus—in evolutionary terms at least—it would be to reproduce and spread efficiently, thereby increasing the likelihood of its own survival. Yet the following is a *verbatim* posting that appeared on Facebook three months after the initial novel coronavirus shutdown in the U.S. together with calls for distancing and self-isolation:

China spread the disease
Democrats spread the lies.
Media spread the panic.
They (*sic*) crashed the economy.
All to destroy our President.
Remember in November.

This set of statements renders the virus itself and what it touches, including entire cultures and regardless of epidemiological facts, breathtakingly political to achieve explicitly stated partisan ends.

The power of powerlessness is obvious to anyone watching the evening news. On most news broadcasts, viewers can bear witness to disenfranchised outsiders who vent their incapacity through the only outlets available: anger and violence, membership in gangs and terrorist organizations that recruit followers from segments of the population most alienated from society, and dropouts or unemployed youth who can envision little future for themselves beyond drugs or prostitution. Powerlessness creates the worst kind of enemy for those in power and for society in general, namely, people with nothing to lose.

A concept related to powerlessness (the absence of command and control) is victimization. More and more, average Americans see themselves as victims living in a social-media era upon whose electronic pages anyone can verbally rage with allies who think as one and agree to devalue opponents as enemies. Victimization in the age of the internet crosses geographic, social, economic, political, and racial boundaries at the speed of electrons. Pro-lifers imagine themselves to be victims of vile baby killers, but liberated women see themselves as victims of pro-lifers. Anti-vaxxers see themselves as victims of medical deceit that negates self-determination, and, failing herd immunity, those who are vaccinated are potential victims of anti-vaxxer ignorance. The economy is a victim of all those damned illegal immigrants because those people pay no taxes, but industrious citizens are victims of immigrants because they are taking our jobs. Traditional marriage is victim of a pagan gay agenda whose aim is to undermine traditional religious and social values, and LGBTQ individuals are victims of religious fanatics. The wealthy are victims of excessive taxation no matter the current tax rate, and businesses are victims of over-regulation, but states are victims of the Federal government while the government is a victim of foreign (often Asian or Muslim) hoaxes or vendettas. NRA members and gun enthusiasts are victims of gun-control advocates, while dead and injured school children are victims of the assault-weapons lobby. Our rush to claim victimization remains spirited even as the moral and legal positions we defend often suffer from inherent contradictions.

The cacophony of claims to victimhood has more than one adverse consequence. With so many voices clamoring for sympathy or support and claiming injury comes a blurring of the distinction between what is genuine mistreatment and what is not. Muffled or ignored in the confusion are the exploitations of many real men, women, and children with legitimate grievances. Among the categories of true victims are the powerless and disenfranchised, including the mentally ill who wander America's wealthy city streets in shameful, homeless disregard; the working poor who cannot earn a living wage or afford health insurance despite long work hours or multiple jobs; Native Americans with inadequate access to educational opportunities and medical treatment; and immigrants, minorities, or others who have suffered for decades real physical, sexual, or emotional abuse.

The most potent counters to nonsense and illogic, for me, are critical thinking and the scientific method. However, given lousy education regarding either approach, some individuals develop a distorted or simplistic idea about what the discipline of science is or can ever be, often derived from popular and superficial sources, such as sci-fi movies and pulp lit. In reality, the discipline of science rarely yields fully formed truths spontaneously from "Ah-ha" moments of insight but, rather, proceeds through a gradual and sometimes messy, controversy-ridden refinement of alternative hypotheses to converge on approximations, and an eventual consensus among experts about the way the world functions.

During early days of the novel coronavirus pandemic, a family member lamented—for the entertainment of an internet audience—the very idea of a pandemic invented by "so-called science authorities" who advocated shifting and apparently contradictory positions on how to deal with a potentially deadly virus. For example, the initial science and medical advice in the U.S. was that facemasks were not protective against COVID-19, and it was pointless to wear them. Subsequently, U.S. authorities reversed their position and began recommending a facemask, or two, for everyone except infants and a few others when going out in public. Worse still, the case and infection fatality rates (CFR and IFR) were all over the map, depending on a reporting state or entity. In response, my relative's conclusion was that nobody in science knows what they are talking about. The reality, of course, is that the problem resided in my relative's head rather than in the ineptness of science. My relative did not understand how science works.

Science as a methodology does not necessarily yield a straightforward succession of insights or revelations amounting to truth, but is a painstakingly slow and erratic crawl to less uncertainty, which looks like fumbling to folks unfamiliar with the process. No single, "true" CFR or IFR value was calculated for COVID-19 during early months of the pandemic because so many population variables (age, wealth, health status, race, location, number of participants, etc.) contributed to and confounded the estimates. No single data point from scientific studies confirms climate change. Some individuals are, nevertheless, too impatient to value nonmagical explanations about science or anything else.

Those who appreciate the value of logic and science, at least to some extent, are not without culpability. During the early AIDS years, I warned many otherwise well-informed friends—drawing from my background in physiology—if they continued to engage in unprotected sex, they were at risk of infection and death. Almost all of them succumbed during the next few years to the disease. Individuals who refused to wear masks and physically distance themselves in the era of COVID-19, scoffing at the advice of virtually all subject-matter experts in the fields of epidemiology and health, similarly risked the health of themselves and others.

There are those who have a willingness to appreciate science for what it is, and others who never will; there are those who believe polar ice fields are enlarging or shrinking, those who would build walls and others who would take walls down. Living just down the street from the wealthiest victimizers are the poorest and most disenfranchised victims of our society; living among us all are magical thinkers and diehard realists. Much of the difference between systems of belief, when it comes to how we treat each other, it seems to me, boils down to education and varying degrees of open-mindedness and compassion, which is roughly equal to the degree of empathy and concern we feel about our frequently irrational, often brilliant, sometimes idiotic, overpopulating brothers and sisters.

Acknowledgements

To Ben Tyrrell at Steel Toe Books I express my gratitude for his remarkably meticulous reviews of the manuscript and for providing insightful suggestions and commentary. Thanks to Dr. Michael Shermer of The Skeptics Society for his critical contributions and annotations to the section on conspiracy theories. My appreciation to Dr. Susan Bentley–Jonason, M.D., Ph.D., and Dr. Kim. R. Jonason, Ph.D., for their friendship over the years, reviews, and well-considered amendments in the right places to the essay on American exceptionalism and elsewhere. Thank you as well, Dr. Karen Thatcher-Britton-Gould, M.D., Ph.D., and Dr. Heidi Goetz, M.D., for encouraging me to remain true to my better convictions regarding what to write and how to write it. Many others, including friends and family members, contributed ideas and inspiration in ways known and unknown to them, without which this book would not be what it is. Finally but not least, I extend my appreciation to Xhenet Aliu for awarding my manuscript the 2020 Steel Toe Books Prize in Prose and for her generous assessment of the book's content.

The following works, some with modifications for this collection, were first published in literary journals or reviews, as follows:

"iWater," winner of the Fulton Prize, in *The Adirondack Review* (Winter 2016).

"A Bomb in the Final Essay by Oliver Sacks," winner of the Editor's Prize, in *Chautauqua, Invention & Discovery* (June 2017).

"American Exceptionalism," *Oyster River Pages* 2 (2018).

"A Personal History of the "F" Word," Honorable Mention, *New Millennium Writings* 42nd Literary Awards, also published by *Fleas On the Dog* (Canada) 2, (April 2019), https://fleasonthedog.com.

"Exercise," *Headland Journal* (New Zealand) 3 (July 2015).

"Extrapolation," *The Broke Bohemian* 5 (Spring 2018), www.brokebohemian.com/new-blog-1/2018/4/6/extrapolation.

"Nine Other Lives," *Parhelion Literary Magazine* (November 1, 2018).

"Maybe Three People," an ArtPrize winning essay, in *Imagine This! An ArtPrize Anthology*, Great Lakes Commonwealth of Letters & Cascade Writers Group 3 (September 2015).

"Paronomasia, Op. 5," *Gravel* (April 2014).

"Post Hoc Ergo Propter Hoc," *The HitchLit Review* 2.1 (July 2018).

"Countering Semantic Poison," *Bending Genres* 10 (August 6, 2019), https://bendinggenres.com/2019/08/06/countering-semantic-poison/.

"Truth, as in Fire and Smoke," *The Transnational, A Literary Magazine* 4 (May 23, 2016), http://www.amazon.com/The-Transnational-Vol-4/

"Conspiracy Theories: Why We Can't Unsee Patterns—Real of Imagined—Once We See Them," *Skeptic* 25(4) (2020).

Neuropsychologist Robert D. Kirvel taught as Psychology Department Head at Montana State University, Billings, before moving to Northern California to start a career in science writing. His writing, on topics ranging from dark matter and climate change to chromosome painting and bioterrorism, has earned him recognition by the National Science and Technology Council, Executive Office of the President of the United States (Obama). His literary works have appeared in four dozen journals and anthologies, and have been published in the U.S., Canada, the U.K., Ireland, New Zealand, and Germany. In addition to winning the Steel Toe Book Award in Prose for *iWater and Other Convictions*, he has received the Chautauqua Editor's Prize for nonfiction, the Fulton Prize for the Short Story, the ArtPrize for creative nonfiction, and two Pushcart nominations. He resides in the progressive San Francisco Bay Area and spends family time at a remote Montana cabin overlooking the Livingston Range of Waterton–Glacier International Peace Park.

REFERENCES

1. Ashraf H. A. Rushdy, "Reflections on Indexing My Lynching Book," *Michigan Quarterly Review 52*, no. 2 (2014), http://hdl. handle.net/2027/spo.act2080.0053.203.

2. Anna Freud, *The Ego and the Mechanisms of Defense* (London: Karnac Books Ltd., 1937).

3. Donald O. Hebb, *The Organization of Behavior* (New York: Wiley and Sons, 1949).

4. Leon Festinger, *A Theory of Cognitive Dissonance* (Stanford, CA: Stanford University Press, 1957).

5. Charles Darwin, *The Expression of the Emotions in Man and Animals*, 3rd ed. (London: Harper Collins, 1998).

6. Yoel Inbar, David A. Pizarro, and Paul Bloom, "Conservatives Are More Easily Disgusted Than Liberals," *Cognition and Emotion* 23, no. 4 (2009): 714–725, http://dx.doi. org/10.1080/02699930802210007.

7. John A. Terrizzi, N. J. Shook, and W. L. Ventis, "Disgust: A Predictor of Social Conservatism and Prejudicial Attitudes Toward Homosexuals," *Personality and Individual Differences* 49, no. 6 (October 2010): 587–592, https://doi.org/10.1016/j. paid.2010.05.024.

8. Woo-Young Ahn, Kenneth T. Kishida, Xiaosi Gu, Terry Lohrenz, Ann Harvey, John R. Alford, Kevin B. Smith, Gideon Yaffe, John R. Hibbing, Peter Dayan, and P. Read Montague, "Nonpolitical Images Evoke Neural Predictors of Political Ideology," *Current Biology* 24, no. 22 (October 2014): 2693–2699, https://doi.org/10.1016/j.cub.2014.09.050.

9. Richard L Gregory, *Eye and Brain: The Psychology of Seeing*, 5th ed. with corrections (Oxford UK: Oxford University Press, 2007), 1–296.

10. Jonathon Haidt, *The Righteous Mind; Why Good People are Divided by Politics and Religion* (New York: Vintage Books, January 2013). See also https://www. ted.com/talks/jonathan_haidt_on_the_moral_mind?language=en.

11. Nicholas Wade, "Race Has a Biological Basis. Racism Does Not," *The Wall Street Journal* (June 22, 2014), https://www.wsj.com/articles/nicholas-wade-race-has-a-biological-basis-racism-does-not-1403476865.

12. Eliza Sankar–Gorton, "The Surprising Science of Race and Racism," *Huffpost Science* (July 14, 2015), http://www.huffingtonpost.com/2015/06/30/racism-race-explained-science-anthropologist_n_7687842.html.

13. Ernst Friedrich Schumacher, *Small is Beautiful* (London: Blond & Briggs Ltd., 1973).

14. Thomas Singer, M.D., "Trump and the American Collective Psyche," in *The Dangerous Case of Donald Trump*, ed. Bandy X. Lee, M.D., M.Div. (New York: St. Martin's Press, 2017), 281–297.

15. Abigail Marsh, *The Fear Factor: How One Emotion Connects Altruists, Psychopaths, and Everyone In-Between* (New York: Basic Books, 2017).

16. Sir Arthur S. Eddington, "Reality, Causation, Science and Mysticism," in *The Nature of the Physical World* (Cambridge at the University Press, 1948), 273–343.

17. Lord Francis Bacon, *Novum Organum or True Suggestions for the Interpretation of Nature*, Part XLVI (New York: P.F. Collier, 1902, original ed. 1620), https://oll.libertyfund.org/title/bacon-novum-organum.

18. Will Durant and Ariel Durant, *The Lessons of History* (New York: Simon and Schuster, 1968), 31, 81–86.

19. Henri Bergson, *The Evolution of Life—Mechanism and Theory* (New York: Henry Holt and Company, 1911).

20. Auguste Comte, *The Positive Philosophy* (New York: Calvin Blanchard, 1858), 27.

21. Jonas T. Kaplan, Sarah I. Gimbel, and Sam Harris, "Neural Correlates of Maintaining One's Political Beliefs in the Face of Counterevidence," *Scientific Reports* 6, no. 39589 (December 2016), https://doi.org/10.1038/srep39589.

22. Giacomo Rizzolatti, Luciano Fadiga, Vittorio Gallese, and Leonardo Fogassi, "Premotor Cortex and the Recognition of Motor Actions," *Cognitive Brain Research* 3, no. 2 (1996): 131–141, https://doi.org/10.1016/0926-6410(95)00038-0.

23. Tania Singer, Ben Seymour, John O'Doherty, Holger Kaube, Raymond J. Dolan, and Chris D. Firth, "Empathy for Pain Involves the Affective but Not Sensory Component of Pain," *Science* 303, no. 5661 (2004): 1157–62, https://doi.org10.1126/science.1093535.

24. Mbemba Jabbi, Marte Swart, and Christian Keysers, "Empathy for Positive and Negative Emotions in the Gustatory Cortex," *Neuroimage* 3, no. 4 (February 2007): 1744–53, https://doi.org/10.1016/j.neuroimage.2006.10.032.

25. Hyeonjin Jeon and Seung-Hwan Lee, "From Neurons to Social Beings; Short Review of the Mirror Neuron System Research and Its Socio-Psychological and Psychiatric Implications," *Clinical Psychopharmacology and Neuroscience* 16, no. 1 (2018): 18–31, https://doi.org/10.9758/cpn.2018.16.1.18.

26. Claus Lamm and Jasminka Majdandzic´, "The Role of Shared Neural Activations, Mirror Neurons, and Morality in Empathy—A Critical Comment," *Neuroscience Research* 90 (2015): 15–24, https://doi.org/10.1016/j.neures.2014.10.008.

27. Lindsay M. Oberman, Jaime A. Pineda, and Vilayanur S. Ramachandran, "The Human Mirror Neuron System: A Link Between Action Observation and Social Skills," *Social Cognitive and Affective Neuroscience* 2, no. 1 (March 2007): 62–66, https://doi.org/10.1093/scan/nsl022.

28. Cigdem V. Sirin, Nicholas A. Valentino, and José D. Villalobos, "Group Empathy Theory: The Effect of Group Empathy on U.S. Intergroup Attitudes and Behavior in the Context of Immigration Threats," *The Journal of Politics* 78, no. 3 (June 2016): 893–908, https://doi.org/10.1086/685735.

29. Cigdem V. Sirin, Nicholas A. Valentino, and José D. Villalobos, "The Social Causes and Political Consequences of Group Empathy," *Political Psychology* 38, no. 3 (June 2017): 427–48, https://doi.org/10.1111/pops.12352.

30. University of South Carolina, "This is Your Brain on Politics: Neuroscience Reveals Brain Differences Between Republicans and Democrats," *ScienceDaily* (November 2012), www. sciencedaily.com/releases/2012/11/121101105003.htm.

31. Yossi Hasson, Maya Tamir, and Kea S. Brahms, "Are Liberals and Conservatives Equally Motivated to Feel Empathy Toward Others?" *Personality and Social Psychology Bulletin* 44, no. 10 (2018): 1449–59, https://doi.org/10.1177/0146167218769867.

32. Elizabeth N. Simas, Scott Clifford, and Justin H. Kirkland, "How Emphatic Concern Fuels Political Polarization," *American Political Science Review* 114, no. 1 (2020): 258–69, https://doi. org/10.1017/S0003055419000534.

33. Justin Kruger and David Dunning, "Unskilled and Unaware of It: How Difficulties in Recognizing One's Own Incompetence Lead to Inflated Self-Assessments," *Journal of Personality and Social Psychology* 77, no. 6 (December 1999): 1121–34, https://doi. org/10.1037//0022-3514.77.6.1121.

34. Christopher Hertzog and A. Emanuel Robinson, "Metacognition and Intelligence," in *Handbook of Understanding and Measuring Intelligence*, eds. O. Wilhelm and R. W. Engle (Thousand Oaks, CA: Sage Publications, Inc., 2005): 101–123, https://doi. org/10.4135/9781452233529.n7.

35. Mayo Clinic Staff, *Gluten-Free Diet* (December 19, 2019), https:// www.mayoclinic.org/healthy-lifestyle/nutrition-and-healthy-eating/in-depth/gluten-free-diet/art-20048530.

36. Robert H. Shmerling, "Right Brian/Left Brain," *Harvard Health Publishing*, Harvard Medical School (November 2019), (https://www.health.harvard.edu/blog/right-brainleft-brain-right-2017082512222).

37. Jared A. Nielsen, Brandon A. Zielinski, Michael A. Ferguson, Janet E. Lainhart, and Jeffrey S. Anderson, "An Evaluation of the Left-Brain vs. Right-Brain Hypotheses with Resting State Functional Connectivity MRI," *PLoS One* 8, no.8 (August 2013), https://doi.org/10.1371/journal.pone.0071275.

38. Michael Shermer, "Why People Believe Conspiracy Theories," *Skeptic* 25, no. 1 (2020), https://bit.ly/2HLz7iR.

39. Marc Pauly, "Conspiracy Theories," *Internet Encyclopedia of Philosophy, A Peer-Reviewed Academic Resource* (2020), https://iep.utm.edu/conspira/.

40. Jan-Willem van Prooijen and Karen M. Douglas, "Belief in Conspiracy Theories: Basic Principles of an Emerging Research Domain," *European Journal of Social Psychology* 48, no. 7 (2018): 897–908, https://doi.org/10.1002/ejsp.2530.

41. Chapman University, "What Aren't They Telling Us?" *Chapman University Survey of American Fears* (October 11, 2016), https://bit.ly/2HPABc0.

42. Eric W. Weisstein, "Ramsey Theory," *MathWorld—A Wolfram Web Resource* (2020), https://bit.ly/2Gs0HB4.

43. Paul Hoffman, *The Man Who Loved Only Numbers: The Story of Paul Erdos and the Search for Mathematical Truth* (New York: Hyperion, 1998), 5–57.

44. Alexander Soifer, ed., *Ramsey Theory: Yesterday, Today, and Tomorrow* (New York: Springer, 2011).

45. See the definition of pareidolia, e.g., https://en.wikipedia.org/wiki/Pareidolia.

46. Michael Shermer, *The Believing Brain* (New York: Henry Holt, 2011).

47. For a brief history of the signal-detection problem in the context of the replication crisis in science, see Stuart Ritchie, *Science Fictions: How Fraud, Bias, Negligence, and Hype Undermine the Search for Truth* (New York: Metropolitan Books, 2020).

48. David Ingle, "Two Visual Systems in the Frog," *Science* 181, no. 4104 (1973): 1053–55, https://doi.org/10.1126/science.181.4104.1053.

49. David H. Hubel, and Torsten N. Wiesel, "Receptive Fields of Single Neurons in the Cat's Striate Cortex," *The Journal of Physiology* 148 (1959): 574–91, https://doi.org/10.1113/jphysiol.1959.sp006308.

50. David H. Hubel, and Torsten N. Wiesel, "Receptive Cells in Striate Cortex of Very Young, Visually Inexperienced Kittens," *Journal of Neurophysiology*, 26 (1963): 994–1002, https://doi.org/10.1152/jn.1963.26.6.994.

51. Christof Koch, *The Quest for Consciousness: A Neurobiological Approach* (New York: Roberts and Co, 2004).

52. Eric Kandel, *The Disordered Mind: What Unusual Brains Tell Us About Ourselves* (New York: Farrar, Straus and Giroux, 2018).

53. Sarah Bate, *Face Recognition and Its Disorders* (New York: Palgrave, 2012).

54. Jan-Willem Van Prooijen, "An Existential Threat Model of Conspiracy Theories," *European Psychologist* 25 (2020): 16–25, https://bit.ly/33n5e0G.

55. Zack Stanton, "You're Living in the Golden Age of Conspiracy Theories," *Politico* (June 17, 2020), https://politi.co/33mgydG.

56. Joseph E. Uscinski and Joseph M. Parent, *American Conspiracy Theories* (New York: Oxford University Press, 2014).

57. Adam M. Enders, and Steven M. Smallpage, "Who Are Conspiracy Theorists? A Comprehensive Approach to Explaining Conspiracy Beliefs," *Social Science Quarterly* 100, no. 6 (August 2019), https://doi.org/10.1111/ssqu.12711.

58. Michael Shermer, "Conspiracies and Conspiracy Theories: What We Should and Shouldn't Believe—and Why," *Audible Original* (2019), https://amzn.to/2Sm2gDa.

59. Andreas Goreis and Martin Voracek, "A Systematic Review and Meta-Analysis of Psychological Research on Conspiracy Beliefs," *Frontiers in Psychology* 11 (February 2019), https://doi.org/10.3389/fpsyg.2019.00205.

60. J. Eric Oliver and Thomas J. Wood, "Conspiracy Theories and the Paranoid Style(s) of Mass Opinion," *American Journal of Political Science* 58, no. 4 (2014): 952–66, https://www.jstor.org/stable/24363536. See also: J. Eric Oliver, "The Science of Conspiracy Theories and Political Polarization," *University of Chicago News*, Big Brains podcast (2020), https://bit.ly/3cTzvav.

61. Joseph E. Uscinski, ed., *Conspiracy Theories and the People Who Believe Them* (Oxford, England: Oxford University Press, 2018).

62. Karen M. Douglas, Joseph E. Uscinski, Robbie M. Sutton, Aleksandra Cichocka, Turkay Nefes, Chee Siang Ang, and Farzin Deravi, "Understanding Conspiracy Theories," *Advances in Political Psychology* 40, no. 1 (2019), https://doi.org/10.1111/pops.12568.

63. CDC Fact Sheet: "HIV Among Gay and Bisexual Men," accessed March 9, 2021, https://www.cdc.gov/nchhstp/newsroom/docs/factsheets/cdc-msm-508.pdf.

64. UNAIDS, Global HIV and AIDS Statistics—2020 Fact Sheet, copyright 2021, https://www.unaids.org/en/resources/factsheet.

65. Oliver Sacks, *The Mind's Eye* (New York: Vintage Books, 2011).

66. Carl Sagan, *The Demon-Haunted World* (New York: Ballantine Books, 1997).

67. Paul R. Ehrlich, *The Population Bomb* (New York: Sierra Club/Ballantine Books, 1968).

68. Viviane Richter, "What Came First, Cells or Viruses?" *COSMOS* (October 19, 2015), https://cosmosmagazine.com/biology/what-came-first-cells-or-viruses/.